AFTER KINSHIP

This innovative book takes a fresh look at the anthropology of kinship and the comparative study of relatedness. Kinship has historically been central to the discipline of anthropology, but what sort of future does it have? What is the impact of recent studies of reproductive technologies, of gender, and of the social construction of science in the West? What significance does public anxiety about the family, or new family forms in the West, have for anthropology's analytic strategies? The study of kinship has rested on a distinction between the "biological" and the "social." But recent technological developments have made this distinction no longer self-evident. What does this imply about the comparison of kinship institutions cross-culturally? Janet Carsten gives an approachable and original view of the past, present, and future of kinship in anthropology. Her observations will be of interest not just to anthropologists but to social scientists generally.

Janet Carsten is Professor of Social and Cultural Anthropology at the University of Edinburgh. She edited *Cultures of Relatedness: New Approaches to the Study of Kinship*, published by Cambridge University Press in 2000, and coedited *About the House: Lévi-Strauss and Beyond* with Stephen Hugh Jones in 1995.

NEW DEPARTURES IN ANTHROPOLOGY

New Departures in Anthropology is a book series that focuses on emerging themes in social and cultural anthropology. With original perspectives and syntheses, authors introduce new areas of inquiry in anthropology, explore developments that cross disciplinary boundaries, and weigh in on current debates. Every book illustrates theoretical issues with ethnographic material drawn from current research or classic studies, as well as from literature, memoirs, and other genres of reportage. The aim of the series is to produce books that are accessible enough to be used by college students and instructors, but also will stimulate, provoke, and inform anthropologists at all stages of their careers. Written clearly and concisely, books in the series are designed equally for advanced students and a broader audience of readers, inside and outside academic anthropology, who want to be brought up to date on the most exciting developments in the discipline.

After Kinship

JANET CARSTEN
University of Edinburgh

PUBLISHED BY THE PRESS SYNDICATE OF THE UNIVERSITY OF CAMBRIDGE
The Pitt Building, Trumpington Street, Cambridge, United Kingdom

CAMBRIDGE UNIVERSITY PRESS
The Edinburgh Building, Cambridge CB2 2RU, UK
40 West 20th Street, New York, NY 10011-4211, USA
477 Williamstown Road, Port Melbourne, VIC 3207, Australia
Ruiz de Alarcón 13, 28014 Madrid, Spain
Dock House, The Waterfront, Cape Town 8001, South Africa

http://www.cambridge.org

First published 2004

Printed in the United States of America

Typeface Minion 10.5/15 pt.　　*System* LATEX 2ε　[TB]

A catalog record for this book is available from the British Library.

Library of Congress Cataloging in Publication Data

Carsten, Janet.
After kinship / Janet Carsten.
　p.　cm. – (New departures in anthropology)
Includes bibliographical references and index.
ISBN 0-521-66198-6 – ISBN 0-521-66570-1 (pbk.)
1. Kinship.　2. Kin recognition.　I. Title.　II. Series.
GN487.C37 2004
306.83–dc21　　　　2003053191

ISBN 0 521 66198 6 hardback
ISBN 0 521 66570 1 paperback

For Jonathan and Jessica

Contents

Acknowledgments

One of the great pleasures of finishing a piece of writing that has taken longer than planned to complete is finding ways to say thank you to those whose support has made the task easier. This book was conceived a long time ago, and I am grateful to Steve Gudeman and Charles Stafford, who first encouraged me to write a book about the "new kinship." Over several years, they, along with Jonathan Spencer, Sarah Franklin, and a number of others, have contributed much-needed positive reinforcement, which has enabled me to see this project through.

Originally, this book was planned as a kind of companion volume and expansion of my introduction to *Cultures of Relatedness* (Carsten 2000a). Although in the end this plan was somewhat overtaken by events, readers will find many parallels between the themes in these two books – including the intellectual debts that I acknowledge here. David Schneider's work forms a running thread through all the chapters. But I have learned most of the anthropology I know from Maurice Bloch and Marilyn Strathern – who for quite different reasons may disagree with parts of what follows. My discussion of personhood in Chapter 4 owes a great deal to conversations with Maurice Bloch, and especially to his article on "Death and the Concept of the Person," published in 1988. The title, *After Kinship*, is of course playful; the message of this book appears to be that "after kinship" is – well, just more kinship (even if it might be of a slightly different kind). But it is also a serious gesture of acknowledgment

Acknowledgments

for the inspiration that Marilyn Strathern's work has provided over many years.

I began writing this book under the auspices of a Nuffield Social Science Research Fellowship. I am grateful to the Nuffield Foundation, and to my colleagues in the Department of Social Anthropology at the University of Edinburgh, for allowing me time off in 1997–8 to write, and conduct research on adoption reunions. I particularly thank Jennifer Speirs for her help in initiating my research on adoption reunions, and the staff of the agency that helped in contacting those whom I interviewed as part of this research. I have kept this organization and those interviewed anonymous in order to protect the latter's privacy.

A somewhat different and longer version of Chapter 5 was published under the title "Substantivism, Antisubstantivism, and Anti-Antisubstantivism" in *Relative Values: Reconfiguring Kinship Studies*, edited by Sarah Franklin and Susan McKinnon (Duke University Press, 2001). I am grateful to Tony Good, Sarah Franklin, and Susan McKinnon for their comments on an earlier version of this chapter. Some of the material on adoption reunions in Chapter 6 was used to a different purpose in my article "'Knowing Where You've Come From': Ruptures and Continuities of Time and Kinship in Narratives of Adoption Reunions," *Journal of the Royal Anthropological Institute* 6: 687–703, 2000. I am grateful to the Royal Anthropological Institute of Great Britain and Ireland and the editors and publishers of this material for permission to use it here.

I am conscious of a greater than usual debt to those whose editing work has made such a substantial contribution to the clarity and coherence of what follows. Steve Gudeman, Michael Lambek, and Jonathan Spencer have given me the benefit of extremely detailed and constructive comments on the first draft of the manuscript. I have tried to follow their advice, and the remaining failings are of course entirely my own. Sally Laird will recognize her influence in my depiction of the Carsten household in London.

Acknowledgments

Much of this book has been written in the shadow of a profound loss. My father, Francis Carsten, died in June 1998. Not long before his death, I discovered a surprising bit of kinship knowledge. As part of his Communist Party activism in the late 1920s and early 1930s, Francis had given talks on Friedrich Engels' *Origins of the Family, Private Property and the State* to study groups in working-class neighborhoods of Berlin. From him I learned not to take kinship for granted, that relationships worth their salt are made rather than given, and that the unconditional gifts of love and support that are their true mark are both enduring and utterly irreplaceable.

Jonathan Spencer and Jessica Spencer have lived with the writing of this book. Apart from many other contributions, they have helped me to see that the givenness of kinship can be a restorative and creative force.

ONE

Introduction: After Kinship?

Nineteen-ninety-five, Nottinghamshire, England. Stephen Blood, critically ill with bacterial meningitis, lies in a coma on life support machines. His sperm are removed without his prior written consent. Within a few days he is dead. Although he and his wife, Diane Blood, had been trying to conceive a child before his death, the British Human Fertilisation and Embryology Authority (HFEA) refuses to grant permission for Diane Blood to undergo artificial insemination using her husband's sperm. Diane Blood challenges the decision in the High Court. In October 1996 the challenge is dismissed on the same grounds as the original HFEA ruling.

Diane Blood announces her intention to take the ruling to the Court of Appeal: "I think that I have the most right of anybody to my husband's sperm and I desperately wanted his baby" (*The Guardian* 18.10.96). Sir Stephen Brown, president of the High Court's Family Division, comments sympathetically, "My heart goes out to this applicant who wishes to preserve an essential part of her late beloved husband. The refusal to permit her so to do is for her in the nature of a double bereavement. It stirs the emotions and evokes what I believe to be universal sympathy for the applicant." "Leading fertility expert" Lord Winston describes the decision of the High Court as "cruel and unnatural." Baroness Warnock, chair of the Parliamentary Committee that led to the setting up of the HFEA, reportedly blames herself: "We didn't think of the kind of contingency which has actually arisen" (*The Guardian* 18.10.96).

November 1996. The HFEA rules that Diane Blood cannot legally export her husband's sperm to Belgium for use there. Once again, the Authority cites the lack of written consent as grounds for this decision. Reports emphasize the conflict between the views of the clinicians seeking to help "sometimes desperate individuals to fulfil themselves through having children" and "the inhuman general ethical principles that get in the way" (*The Guardian* 23.11.96).

February 1997. An Appeal Court judgment upholds Diane Blood's right as a European Community citizen to have medical treatment in another member state. She is granted permission to export her husband's sperm to Belgium and to have treatment there. At the same time, the Appeal Court preempts the possibility of further similar applications by ruling that the extraction and storage of the sperm without Stephen Blood's consent had been unlawful. Professor Ian Craft, director of the London Gynaecology and Infertility Centre, calls the decision a "fudge," blaming a "restrictive" and "intransigent" HFEA. Pointing out that women have the right to undergo termination of a pregnancy or a hysterectomy without their partner's permission, he argues that preventing a woman from becoming pregnant in such circumstances is an infringement of individual freedom (*The Guardian* 7.2.97).

Nineteen-nineties Israel.[1] A series of rabbinic debates on artificial insemination are conducted with unusual intensity. The debates focus on three main issues: Can sperm for artificial insemination be procured from Jews, given that masturbation is prohibited under Halakha (Jewish religious law)? What is the relation between a sperm donor and a child

[1] This account is closely based on Susan Kahn's work, *Reproducing Jews: A Cultural Account of Assisted Conception in Israel* (2000).

conceived using his sperm? And what is the status of the child conceived in this way (Kahn 2000: 94–7)?

The orthodox rabbinate reaches some unexpected conclusions. Discussions take into account the prohibition on masturbation for orthodox Jewish men; the problematic status of a child conceived by means of donated Jewish sperm, who could be considered to have an equivalent status to that of a child born from an adulterous relation between a married Jewish woman and a Jewish man not her husband; and the further possibility that such a child might eventually, unknowingly, enter an incestuous marriage with a half sibling. The rabbinate rules that, in the light of these complications, where male infertility is not treatable, donor sperm must be taken from non-Jewish men (2000: 104–10). Here procurement is deemed unproblematic since non-Jews are not bound by the Halakhic prohibition on masturbation. Similarly, the adulterous connotations of the union of egg and sperm are obviated since, according to Halakhic proscriptions covering Jews, only relationships between Jews can be defined as adulterous. But what is perhaps most satisfying for those concerned is that the use of non-Jewish sperm does not affect the Jewish identity of the child since Jewishness is inherited from the mother. Like children born to a Jewish mother and a non-Jewish father, a baby conceived through the union of a "Jewish egg" with "non-Jewish sperm" is defined under these rulings as a Jewish baby.

This erasure of non-Jewish sperm is so complete that, according to these rulings, children born to different Jewish mothers by means of non-Jewish sperm taken from the same donor are quite unrelated. Marriage between adults so conceived is permitted because the sperm necessary for their conception has apparently had no part in forming their identity (2000: 104–5). This is one of a number of selective erasures accomplished in a highly conscious manner and in the particular political context of the modern state of Israel – a country with "more fertility clinics per capita than any other in the world," where the full range of modern fertility treatments is subsidized by state health insurance, and where every citizen, "regardless of religion or marital status, is eligible for unlimited rounds of in vitro fertilization treatment" until the birth of two live children (2000: 2). In Israel, the reproduction of Jews is a vital concern, and regulations governing fertility treatment, like marriage and divorce law, are grounded in and informed by Jewish law (2000: 76). The seemingly arcane discussions of Orthodox rabbis over what constitutes a Jew thus have a direct political salience – reproduction of family and nation could hardly be more closely intertwined.

∽

Nineteen-ninety-three Scotland.[2] Anna, a married woman in her thirties, adopted as a baby, is anxiously preparing for her first meeting with her birth mother. As she recalled in an interview a few years later:

I'm on a high. I'd just been out and I'd bought myself a new jumper. I thought, I'll wear my trouser suit and this new jumper to meet her. I had it all planned out – I didn't want to look too dressy; I didn't want to look too scruffy. I just wanted to look in-between, because I had this idea that maybe she was quite poor. . . .

But what has precipitated this meeting awaited with so much trepidation? Amidst a wealth of childhood and teenage experiences that she summarizes as "like living in a house of people who are aliens," Anna selects two particular events. As a child of about eight, she recalls how:

. . . one day, I was upstairs in my bedroom, and I heard my mum talking to my uncle David, and all I heard my uncle David saying was "one day Anna will probably ask you something about who her mum is. I'm sure she'll ask you when she's older." And that was the only night I wet my bed, and I cried my heart out. The only time I can remember crying, really crying.

---

[2] Names and some other details in this account have been changed. The background to this research is explained in Chapter 4.

But then she says, "It wasn't a big deal. I always wondered why she gave me away but I never had the courage to go and ask any questions." The second event Anna picks out occurs about ten years later: "I was playing a game. It wasn't a game. I was playing with friends – the ouija board. And I got a horrible message about my mother, telling me horrible names and things. It really upset me. . . . That's what made me ask my mum."

Some years later, as the mother of two children, Anna decided to initiate a search for her birth mother. She enlisted the help of an adoption agency, which advised her about accessing first her original birth certificate, and then the court records of her adoption:

It was just so amazing, it was like looking in a book and reading about yourself. It was all right at the time. But when I went to bed at night I realised I couldn't sleep. It was so much for me to take in. I even found out what my name was. I remember thinking I had no idea that I had a different name.

After she had made several unsuccessful phone calls to people of the same name picked out of the phone book, the agency advising Anna located the brother of her birth mother, and she sent him a letter. Two days later, and as she put it, "on a high," she received a letter back: "I sat down, and I had my cup of tea and my Mars bar and I'm so excited. . . ."

The outcome to this story was not the reunion anticipated with such excitement. The letter revealed that Anna's mother – who had herself made repeated but unsuccessful attempts to contact her daughter – had died not long before Anna had initiated her search. Although this discovery triggered an immense emotional upheaval, Anna did eventually establish contact and relationships with members of her birth mother's family.

But even when finding a birth mother is possible, establishing a relationship is by no means a certainty. Another person I spoke to described his first meeting with his birth mother in this way: "There's definitely no 'ting,' connection, like that, because this is somebody you don't know.

You don't know this person, it's a total stranger. It might not have been my mother, she could have sent somebody else."

Redoing Kinship

I have chosen just three vignettes to illustrate some of the many new guises taken by kinship at the close of the twentieth century and the beginning of the twenty-first. What are these stories about? And what do they have in common? This book is conceived, at least in part, as an answer to these questions. Clearly, these sketches reveal concerns with which we are all too familiar – most obviously, the intense, often too intense, emotional experiences that embody family relations. They illustrate too the direct linkages between the enclosed, private world of the family, and the outside world of the state's legislative apparatus and the project of nation-making. They speak to issues of personhood, gender, and bodily substance.

More generally, the stories I have chosen raise questions about the nature of kinship. These questions focus on the extent to which kinship is part of the pregiven, natural order of things and the extent to which it is shaped by human engagement. A central theme of the chapters that follow is the distinction that is made, both in anthropological analyses of kinship and in indigenous folk notions, between what is "natural" in kinship and what is "cultural." Kinship may be viewed as given by birth and unchangeable, or it may be seen as shaped by the ordinary, everyday activities of family life, as well the "scientific" endeavors of geneticists and clinicians involved in fertility treatment or prenatal medicine. In the past, anthropologists have seen the distinction between "social" and "biological" kinship as fundamental to an analytical understanding of this domain. For the most part, anthropologists confined their efforts to understanding the "social" aspects of kinship, setting aside the pregiven and "biological" as falling outside their expertise. But increasingly, this separation, which is undoubtedly central to Western folk understandings of kinship, has itself come under scrutiny. This shift is partly the result of technological developments and the public concerns they engender, although it is also highlighted in many more prosaic contexts that anthropologists encounter.

This book is, in part, an essay on the theme of "what's happened to kinship?" It is about the ways in which our most familiar concepts of kinship are changing. Certainly, many people are confronted in their daily lives and in media representations by some apparently unfamiliar kinds of kinship – not just broken or reconstituted families, but a new world of possibilities engendered by technological interventions. Fertility treatments, genetic testing, posthumous conception, cloning, and the mapping of the human genome seemingly carry the possibility of shaking some fundamental assumptions about familial connection. Taken together with media hype about the "crisis of the family," the endless possibilities offered by new technologies seem to open the door to a brave new world that is indeed "after kinship." But although the chapters that follow analyze kinship in some of its new forms, they also reveal some old concerns. Part of my intention here is to place what is new in the field of kinship in the context of what is more familiar.

I consider the question "what's happened to kinship?" in two quite different senses. Although this book is partly taken up with some striking, and at times bizarre, new possibilities that have become part of the daily currency of experiences of relatedness, I am equally concerned with the analytic strategies by which they may be understood. Since the late nineteenth century, anthropologists have claimed kinship as the area of expertise central to their discipline. And it is as an anthropologist that I examine, among other topics, reunions between adults adopted in infancy and their birth kin, or the legal and ethical discussions surrounding Diane Blood's rights to her husband's sperm, or the debates about sperm donation of the Orthodox rabbinate in Israel. I seek to understand these new developments in the context of an anthropological literature in which crosscultural comparison is the most prominent methodological tool. But I am equally interested in the analytic work that anthropologists do when they draw these comparisons, and in recent developments in the study of kinship in anthropology (cf. Bouquet 1993, 1996, 2000; Strathern 1992c; Franklin and McKinnon 2001a). So, this book is at least as much about what has happened to the anthropological study of kinship in recent years as it is about what has happened to our everyday experience of kinship.

But there is of course a relation between these two concerns, and it is one that I hope will be apparent to the reader of this book. I argue that partly because mid-twentieth century debates about kinship in anthropology became removed from the most obvious facets of actual lived experiences of kinship, kinship as a subdiscipline became increasingly marginal to anthropology through the 1970s and 1980s. Not only did anthropological renditions all too often fail to capture what made kinship such a vivid and important aspect of the experiences of those whose lives were being described, but they also ignored the pressing political concerns of the postcolonial world and of the world immediately outside the academy. It is no surprise, then, that in this era studies of kinship gave way to studies that focused on power and hegemony or on gender.

The close link between, for example, the rise of feminism as a social and political force outside the academy in the 1960s and 1970s and the blossoming of studies of gender in anthropology now seems obvious. And other connections are equally apparent – for example, between the current revitalization of kinship studies and wider public concerns about technological developments in the field of fertility treatment and genetics. However perversely anthropologists might seem to disconnect the actualities of their social and political worlds from their academic renditions of others' lives, inevitably they inform each other.

This book is not however, only about what is new and what is familiar in contemporary kinship. It is also an attempt to set out a new project for the study of kinship. The stories with which I began highlight themes that are central to my argument. Perhaps the most obvious is that of comparison and contrast. Running through all the chapters is an adherence to the comparative endeavor that informs anthropology. Although in many respects the last ten years have witnessed a resurgence in kinship studies, I suggest toward the end of this chapter that the value of comparison has been sidelined. In recent years, anthropologists have focused on local understandings and meanings of kinship rather than crosscultural comparison. In this book, I place not just the close, intimate, and emotional work of kinship beside the larger projects of state and nation, but I also juxtapose examples of kinship taken from North America, Britain, and Poland beside those from Malaysia, Israel, and Madagascar, among other places.

I have already mentioned the close-up, experiential dimension of kinship that too often is excluded from anthropological accounts. This lived experience often seems too mundane or too obvious to be worthy of close scrutiny. But the stories I have sketched make clear that kinship is far from being simply a realm of the "given" as opposed to the "made." It is, among other things, an area of life in which people invest their emotions, their creative energy, and their new imaginings. These of course can take both benevolent and destructive forms. The idea that kinship involves not just rights, rules, and obligations but is also a realm of new possibilities is apparent whether we look at mundane rituals of everyday life – a birthday party or a family meal – the seemingly baroque arguments of Orthodox rabbis, or the decisions reached by the HFEA. This sense of infectious excitement, as well as anxiety, afforded by new possibilities emerges clearly when ordinary people engage with technological innovations. I take it as fundamental that creativity is not only central to kinship conceived in its broadest sense, but that for most people kinship constitutes one of the most important arenas for their creative energy (cf. Faubion 2001).

But why should these points matter? And where do they diverge from kinship in its more classic anthropological renditions? To answer these questions, I turn to some anthropological history, looking first at midtwentieth century anthropological renditions of kinship.

Kinship in the Mid-Twentieth Century

This book is neither intended to be a conventional textbook nor a summary of everything that has happened in the anthropology of kinship over the last thirty years. The history I give here is a partial one that, for convenience, I divide into three phases. In this section, I look back at the anthropology of kinship in the mid-twentieth century. The following section focuses on the culturalist critique of kinship, and particularly on the work of David Schneider. Finally, I take up more recent developments in kinship studies and place them in the context of some contemporary practices of relatedness.

For the leading figures of early and mid-twentieth century British social anthropology – Bronislaw Malinowski, A. R. Radcliffe-Brown, Edward Evans-Pritchard, and Meyer Fortes – kinship was central to the discipline. The reason for this was that these authors were attempting to understand the basis for the orderly functioning of small-scale societies in the absence of governmental institutions and states. They saw kinship as constituting the political structure and providing the basis for social continuity in stateless societies.

This defining paradigm was crucial to the way the field developed. Both Malinowski and Fortes saw the nuclear family as a universal social institution, necessary to fulfill the functions of producing and rearing children (see Malinowski 1930; Fortes 1949). Although both Malinowski and Fortes had a keen interest in domestic family arrangements and in relationships between parents and children, partly because of the influence of Freudian psychology on their work, Fortes (1958) also set out a crucial division between what he called the "domestic" and the "politico-jural" domains of kinship. The former concerned the intimate world of individual nuclear families – mothers, fathers, and their children – and the latter concerned the public roles or offices ordered by wider kinship relations. In a lineage-based society in which the kin group held property, and in which descent from a common ancestor determined membership, decision-making powers over the group were vested in the elders by virtue of the position they held in the lineage. Politics and religion (ancestor worship) could not be separated from kinship, and kinship in turn determined succession to office. The political and religious aspects of kinship were the source of cohesiveness in these societies, and rendered kinship interesting for anthropology.

The social context in which the nuclear family was set – in other words, wider kinship arrangements – varied greatly in different cultural settings. What was of interest for social anthropologists was precisely the variability of kinship institutions, not the part that stayed constant. Thus from early on, the comparative study of kinship was explicitly defined as *not* being about intimate domestic arrangements and the behavior and emotions associated with them. These were assumed to be to a large degree universally constant, or a matter for psychological rather than sociological study (see, for example, Radcliffe-Brown 1950).

This particular construction of what constituted kinship had important implications in terms of gender. In many societies studied by anthropologists, it was women who were most concerned with socializing young children and with organizing and carrying out domestic activities. Thus it followed that women were more or less excluded from anthropological accounts. In the mid-century, British social anthropology was dominated by avowedly ahistorical studies of African "unilineal kinship systems." The lineage, whether organized around descent in the male or the female line (that is, patrilineal or matrilineal), was understood to be the central organizing feature of these systems. Lineages were described as "corporate" in the sense that they functioned as though they were a single property-owning and jural unit. Considerable anthropological labor and analytical skill were deployed in describing the functioning of such systems in terms of a complex typology of "maximal" and "minimal," "lineages" and "sublineages," whose clear boundaries seemed never to be in question (see, for example, Fortes 1953; Fortes and Evans-Pritchard 1940).

In retrospect, it is clear that the unproblematic boundedness of the units described was much more a product of a particular kind of analytic endeavor than a reflection of the much messier realities of the political and social context of colonial and postcolonial Africa (see Kuper 1988; McKinnon 2000). Indeed, these changing realities were increasingly difficult to account for within the synchronic framework of this kind of study. Nor did matters become any easier when descent group theory was transported outside Africa to societies in Southeast Asia or Papua New Guinea, where the notion of a lineage as a corporate group was difficult to apply (see Barnes 1962; Strathern 1992c).

While British kinship studies were largely preoccupied with the analysis of descent groups, in France things took a different turn. Claude Lévi-Strauss's *The Elementary Structures of Kinship* was published in French in 1949, and appeared in English translation in 1969. In it, Lévi-Strauss proposed a grand theory of the development of human culture in which kinship occupied a central role. But this was a very different kind of kinship from its British cousin. Lévi-Strauss was primarily concerned with the logic of culture rather than how societies functioned or what the actual practices of a particular society were. He sought to analyze social rules in terms of their structural relation to each other, rather than their specific content or the extent to which people adhered to them.

Lévi-Strauss treated the existence of social rules determining who was legitimately marriageable as fundamental to human culture. In all cultures, he argued, there were rules delimiting relations that were regarded as too close for marriage. The prohibition against incest was a universal cultural phenomenon, distinguishing the human world from that of animals. The actual content of rules against incest, however, was culturally variable in terms of which particular relations were proscribed. Unlike earlier analyses of incest, Lévi-Strauss's work attempted to account for both the universality of these proscriptions and their variability. He argued that the taboo against incest was an expression of the fundamental cultural necessity for exchange to take place between groups. The incest

taboo ensured that men exchanged women in marriage rather than marrying their sisters, and this in turn set up the categories that differentiated one social group from another. Thus the proscription against incest
marked the first step in the transition from nature to culture.

This part of Lévi-Strauss's theory was formulated in the most general
terms. Incest taboos ensured "exogamy," marriage into other groups, and
generated exchange, which was the prerequisite of culture. But once again
the implications in terms of gender were hardly neutral. Not all exchanges
were equivalent. For Lévi-Strauss, it was men who exchanged women in
marriage. Women were the "supreme gift" – no other gift could be of equal
value because women were necessary to ensure the continuity of the group
through procreation. Later feminist scholars not only took exception to
the terms in which this theory was put, to the objectification of women
involved, but also demonstrated that in many societies marriage cannot
be considered as an exchange between men. In many cultures women take
an active part in arranging marriages, and may indeed take the leading role
in organizing them (see, for example, Peletz 1987; Carsten 1997). Further,
Lévi-Strauss's methods were not always taken up by his followers in the
most subtle manner. The opposition between nature and culture, and
the more general structuralist tendency to understand culture in terms
of paired oppositions with mediating terms between them, sometimes
took the form of rather schematic lists in which women were opposed
to men, nature to culture, the raw to the cooked, and so on. The result
was that women were unproblematically lumped with a set of devalued
terms, which did little to explicate the intricacies of how people actually
experienced their social world.

Lévi-Strauss's work on kinship also contained some complex theorizing on the long-term structural implications of particular types of marriage alliance in which actors are enjoined to marry certain categories
of kin through the existence of "positive marriage rules." Lévi-Strauss
termed such systems "elementary" and contrasted them with "complex"
systems in which there was no positive injunction to marry specific kin

but only "negative marriage rules" that stated who was not marriageable. The same structural principles underlay both types of kinship, but these were obscured in complex structures by the role that factors such as wealth or class played in the choice of a marriage partner. Kinship did not play the same kind of organizing role in complex systems as in elementary ones. These theories sparked a vituperative debate with Lévi-Strauss's Anglo-Saxon colleagues, particularly over whether "alliance" or "descent" was the more fundamental principle in kinship, and on the nature of marriage rules.

Lévi-Strauss's work had a major impact on the study of kinship by shifting attention from relations of descent to those of marriage, and to exchange more generally. In underlining the centrality of marriage in kinship, and pointing to its importance in establishing and maintaining relations between groups, rather than just individuals, Lévi-Strauss established principles that later studies could not ignore. For the analysis of kinship in non-African societies, particularly, Melanesia, South America, and Southeast Asia, this proved particularly fruitful. Furthermore, the idea that marriage was an elaborate, long-term exchange involving the transfer of goods, services, and people that cemented relations between two groups of affines (or "in-laws") was taken on board even by analysts of kinship who would have rejected much else in Lévi-Strauss's theoretical enterprise.

Several decades later, an assessment of the debate between alliance and descent theory can hardly avoid noting that, however forcefully opposed the protagonists were, there was also some common ground between them. In both kinds of analysis, kinship roles were described in highly normative terms. Within a particular culture, it was assumed that the social role of "husband" or "father" allowed for very little variation. Women's roles were often portrayed in an even more standardized way than men's – and this was a result of the way men were perceived as exchanging women in marriage, and the objectification of women entailed. Assumptions about women's lack of political control as well as those about the nature of the domestic family meant that what being a "wife" or "mother" actually involved was not always subject to analytic scrutiny.

Whereas mid-century anthropologists took kinship to be central to social organization in the non-Western societies that they studied, studies of kinship in Western societies by sociologists, historians, and anthropologists tended to assume that kinship was a relatively minor aspect of social organization. Here kinship was seen as divorced from political, economic, and religious life, and more or less reduced to the nuclear family. Although the degree of control women exerted over the household and family was recognized as variable, the family constituted an isolated, private, domestic, and above all "female" domain. Where social scientists or historians investigated kinship in Europe, they tended to view its instrumental aspects – in property relations, inheritance patterns, and economic exchanges – as paramount (see, for example, Goody 1983).

In defining itself as a discipline, anthropology thus reinforced the boundaries between the West and the rest. Kinship was something "they" have; "we" have families, and this was a quite different matter. Feminist scholarship within and beyond anthropology has of course taught us to question the sharp division between private and public, the domain of the family and that of the state (see, for example, Yanagisako 1979; Harris 1981). In different ways, therefore, from the 1970s on, studies of gender necessarily reshaped anthropological understandings of kinship – and this is a story I take up in Chapter 3.

Although I do not pursue this theme here, another important trend in the rereading of kinship, once the debate between alliance and descent no longer seemed so salient, was inspired by the Marxist critique of anthropology in the 1960s and 1970s. Here households or lineages were examined as units of production, and property was seen as the basis of relations (see, for example, Meillassoux 1984; Goody 1990; and, for an overview, Peletz 1995a). If these accounts now seem in some ways reductionist, they nevertheless had the advantage of making property relations and social change central to the anthropological study of kinship.

So far, my summary of the trajectory of kinship studies has concentrated mainly on British and French anthropology. In North America, the comparative study of kinship classification, or relationship terminologies, continued to preoccupy anthropologists from Lewis Henry Morgan (1871) and Alfred Kroeber (1909) right up to the mid-century and beyond (see, for example, Lounsbury 1965; Murdock 1949; Scheffler 1972; 1978; Scheffler and Lounsbury 1972). In this tradition, language was seen as a direct reflection of culture, and kinship terminologies were of interest because they revealed the way that language shaped social categories and hence behavior. Increasingly, however, studies of kin classification became a highly technical and specialized area, quite divorced from the messier realities of social and political processes as well as the everyday experience of kinship.

Points of Departure

This book examines what has happened to kinship through various tropes: the house, gender, personhood, substance, and reproductive technologies. I have chosen these because each of them has been important in an endeavor, which began in the 1970s, of "undoing" kinship in its various classic anthropological guises. These themes have, in many respects, been instrumental in shifting anthropology's center of gravity away from kinship. But each also holds possibilities for refashioning the study of kinship in new ways. And it is to this end that I gather in this book some of the insights learned in these fields.

If the revitalization of kinship studies is an analytic project, the inspiration for it comes from the people whom anthropologists study – from the widespread interest in Diane Blood's story, or the sympathy one might feel listening to Anna's story of her search for her birth mother. When the abstract theoretical debates of mid-twentieth century kinship studies lost sight of the most crucial experiental aspects of everyday relatedness, they could no longer hold the attention of any but the more technically minded scholars. I take it as axiomatic that the creative energy that ordinary people apply to their lived relationships makes this a topic that is anything but boring, abstract, or technical.

A century or more of crosscultural comparison of institutions of kinship has taught anthropologists to take little for granted in the way people live out and articulate notions of kinship. Historical studies suggest that the stable nuclear family of mid-twentieth century Britain or North America was a rather minor historical blip in a much more dynamic and complex *longue durée*. Late marriage as well as high rates of celibacy and of pregnancy outside marriage were prominent patterns of familial life in northern Europe from the middle ages to the nineteenth century. High rates of mortality meant that marriage was often a short-lived relationship – brought to a close, however, not by divorce, as it often is today, but by death. Parental death resulted in complex and mobile residence patterns for children.[3]

The work of historians of the family also suggests that in a world where death, separation, and loss occurred all too frequently, the small rituals of everyday life were less focused on remembering past generations and deceased family members (as they seem to be today) than on forgetting. John Gillis (1997) argues forcefully that the myth of a much more stable family in the past is actually a product of a nineteenth century social sensibility. In the face of profound social change, this myth has been a very powerful force in shaping an imaginary social landscape of stability and continuity. At the beginning of the twenty-first century, however, our vivid consciousness of new forms of family life and new ideas of how

---

[3] I have baldly summarized a wealth of work on the history of the family in northern Europe and North America in a few sentences. Interested readers may want to refer to, for example, Gillis 1985, 1997; Herlihy 1985; Laslett 1977; Seccombe 1992; Stone 1977.

relations should be lived make apparent the creative work demanded from those who live and experience these apparently new ways of being related.

While historians have highlighted the myth of the stable, traditional family, anthropologists' depictions of kinship have often been paradoxically constrained by structural features of the societies that they were describing. David Schneider occupies a pivotal role in the reformulation of kinship studies in anthropology. This is because his work straddled two traditions in the anthropology of kinship. One, which I have already described, focused on the structure and functions of social groups, and the other examined the meanings of kinship within a particular culture. Schneider was the product of a North American tradition in anthropology going back to Morgan (whom I referred to briefly in the previous section) and Franz Boas. This tradition saw culture as essentially language-like, and the study of kinship terminology therefore revealed central aspects of culture. Schneider, however, reacted against the abstract and technical studies of terminological systems of his North American contemporaries as well as the premises on which they were based. Schneider's two main works, *American Kinship* (1980 [1968]) and *A Critique of the Study of Kinship* (1984), founded a new kind of study in the field of kinship. Here the generation of cultural meanings was the central problem, rather than either the functioning of social groups or the comparative analysis of kinship terminologies.

The shift exemplified in Schneider's work was itself part of a larger double move in anthropology from function to meaning. This involved both a departure from British-style studies focusing on social structure, as epitomized by the work of Radcliffe-Brown and Fortes, and also a move away from Lévi-Straussian structuralism. In this disciplinary change of direction, the work of Clifford Geertz was much more influential than that of Schneider. But the intellectual roots of both Schneider and Geertz can also be traced via their teacher Talcott Parsons to a Weberian theory of meaning (cf. Kuper 1999).

Schneider's work thus presents us with a critical juncture in kinship studies as well as a challenge. He laid out why the study of kinship could no longer continue in the way it had before. And he also seemed to point to a new way of doing kinship in anthropology – although, as we shall see, just how this was to be done was sometimes quite problematic and obscure. In the chapters that follow, I have used Schneider's work not just as a starting point, but as a kind of leitmotiv – picking up various threads from his arguments but also using his work to propose some new ways of thinking about kinship.

Schneider's *Critique* was a highly polemical discussion of the place of kinship within anthropology. Indeed, to many observers, it could be reckoned as a comprehensive dismantling of kinship's centrality to the discipline. And this is another reason to focus on Schneider. Famously, along with others in the 1970s (see Needham 1971), Schneider asserted that the analytic domain occupied by kinship was demonstrably unsound. Anthropologists had marked out this domain using folk models derived from their own Euro-American cultures. These models could be shown to be invalid crossculturally. The way forward was to dismantle the separate domains of kinship, politics, religion, and economics into which anthropology had been distributed.[4]

The central theme of both *American Kinship* and *A Critique of the Study of Kinship* was the relationship between nature and culture, or between the biological and social aspects of kinship. Schneider (1980) framed his analysis of *American Kinship* around a distinction between the "order of nature" and the "order of law," or between substance and code. In *A Critique of the Study of Kinship*, he demonstrated that kinship theory was steeped in Euro-American folk assumptions about the primacy of ties derived from sexual procreation, and that these assumptions did not

---

[4] Domaining practices in anthropology have been the subject of much recent analytic attention (see Yanagisako 1979; 1987; Yanagisako and Delaney 1995; McKinnon 2000; Franklin and McKinnon 2001a).

necessarily apply crossculturally. His work thus problematized the relationship between what was apparently biological and what was cultural in kinship. In this way, Schneider opened up a whole field of enquiry, which has been taken up more recently by a number of authors in studies of reproductive technologies, which I turn to in the following section.

On the one hand, then, Schneider's work could be taken to imply that the study of kinship had no future; on the other, by focusing on culture as a symbolic system, he could be seen as establishing a new tradition in the study of kinship. It now seems strange that *American Kinship* should have failed to take account of important sources of variation in how kinship in America is construed, such as gender, power, or ethnicity. But it is also striking that those who have pointed out these deficiencies have themselves been most strongly influenced by Schneider (see, for example, Yanagisako and Delaney 1995).

After Schneider

While the relevance of kinship studies in the 1970s and 1980s seemed to be on the decline, and kinship's typologies looked increasingly worn, studies of gender and of the person came to the fore. These apparently took over some of the domain previously occupied by kinship in anthropology, and thus contributed further to the marginalization of kinship within anthropology. By the late 1980s, however, one could discern that kinship was beginning to undergo something of a renaissance. The rise of symbolic anthropology, influenced by the work of Geertz, had focused attention on symbolic aspects of the person (see, for example, Daniel 1984), while feminism, as I have already noted, had clearly inspired an anthropological interest in gender. But it also became increasingly clear that gender and personhood could not be understood if they were divorced from the kinds of social institutions that anthropologists had previously bracketed under kinship – marriage, family structures, procreation beliefs, inheritance, and so on (see Yanagisako and Collier 1987). In other words, as I discuss in Chapters 3 and 4, studies of gender and personhood began to feed back into kinship, revitalizing it and contributing to a reformulation of what kinship was all about and how it should be studied.

The other main impetus to the rebirth of kinship was provided by developments in reproductive technologies. Techniques such as AID (artificial insemination by donor) and IVF (in vitro fertilization) raised new questions about the nature of motherhood, of fatherhood, and of connections between children and their parents. These questions are central to the vignettes with which I began this chapter. Diane Blood raised widespread sympathy in Britain because she portrayed her own situation as resulting from an "obvious" set of links between parents and children, but her particular predicament had resulted from new technological developments. Similarly, an adoptee's search for a birth parent necessarily raises questions about the possibility of different, multiple connections between parents and children.

As I have mentioned, some of the questions raised by medical innovations were framed in terms of familiar concerns about incest and adultery, which, together with procreation beliefs, had long been of interest to anthropologists. But there were also more profound questions raised by the new technologies, centering on the role of biology, or nature, itself. For the reasons I have already sketched out, Schneider's work was highly relevant here, and has supplied a theoretical groundwork for much of the recent work in this area (see, for example, Strathern 1992a; Franklin 1997, 2001; Franklin and McKinnon 2001a).

Marilyn Strathern (1992a, 1992b), in particular, has used discourses about recent technological developments to question the place of nature not just in kinship, but in wider knowledge practices in Euro-American culture. Her work constitutes another strong influence on this book. Strathern (1992a) takes apart the opposition between a fixed or given nature and a changeable or contingent culture. Nature, she argues, can no longer be considered as the grounding for culture, or as simply there to be revealed or discovered. It is at least partly "produced" through technological intervention, and this involves a "literalization" of what previously had remained implicit in Western concepts of nature – and of kinship. What implications does this have for kinship, or for how knowledge itself is understood? Kinship, Strathern argues, is of particular significance here precisely because, in Euro-American ideas, it has been thought of as a realm where nature and culture interconnect. Nature is of course the necessary ground from which culture emerges, and kinship, like culture, is thought of as being based in nature. Kinship also provides an image of the relation between nature and culture (cf. Strathern 1992a: 87, 198).

While Schneider opened up a field of enquiry – the relation between the biological and the social in kinship – his own work rather curiously failed to resolve the contradiction that he so neatly demonstrated. He himself never quite abandoned the dichotomy between biological and social aspects of kinship, or suggested how this dichotomy might be opened up or reformulated (cf. Carsten 2000a; Franklin 2001; Franklin and McKinnon 2001a). These questions are, however, not just relevant to the study of kinship. They have much wider sociological implications, as Strathern's work makes clear, for Western knowledge practices and for how we view the process of scientific "discovery." It is thus no coincidence that in the field of sociology of science, writers such as Donna Haraway (1989, 1991, 1997) and Bruno Latour (1993) have also focused on the problematic relationship between nature and culture.

The Old and the New

In a curious way, however, the important work I have been discussing has remained somwhat isolated from a more traditionally conceived and comparatively based anthropological study of kinship. Arguably, one effect of the culturalist critique of kinship was that the emphasis on local meanings has tended to impede the classic anthropological project of comparison and contrast. The divergence between studies of the social effects of reproductive technologies and more "mainstream" anthropological studies of kinship in non-Western societies has in part been the result of viewing kinship in terms of local idioms or as a symbolic system.

It is also notable that the division between the "new kinship studies" and the old contrasts sharply with the fruitful dialogue between the field of gender studies and work on reproductive technologies (see, for example, Franklin 1997; Franklin and Ragoné 1998; Ginsburg and Rapp 1991; Ragoné and Twine 2000; Rapp 1999; Yanagisako and Delaney 1995). This mutual dialogue arises from the fact that both the study of gender and that of assisted conception rest on a single project of defamiliarizing the "natural" and that which is taken for granted (see, for example, MacCormack and Strathern 1980; Franklin and McKinnon 2001a).

The study of kinship, however, has tended to be more rigidly divided between "traditionalists" and "revisionists." This trend is well demonstrated in recent textbooks on kinship, whose chapter headings for the most part recapitulate a view of kinship as it was perceived in the 1970s, covering topics such as descent, lineage theory, alliance, the domestic domain, relationship terminology, and so on, with perhaps a final chapter devoted to reproductive technologies (see Holy 1996; Parkin 1997).[5]

The divide between these two tendencies in the study of kinship is replicated and reinforced by a further separation in the geographic locus for these two kinds of study. While ethnographic studies that focus on recent technological developments, or new forms of kinship, have often been based on the West (see, for example, Modell 1994; Ragoné 1994; Franklin 1997; Weston 1991; Rapp 1999; Edwards 2000), the more traditional kind of kinship study has tended to be located in non-Western cultures, and often in rural communities.

---

[5] An interesting exception to this trend is Linda Stone's *Kinship and Gender: An Introduction*, (1997) which places gender at the center of what might otherwise be a conventional kinship textbook.

This book was conceived as an attempt to reintegrate these two trends. Here I align myself with a number of recent volumes on kinship that, in different ways, draw on the insights of Schneider, but rather than jettison kinship, take up his challenge to redefine it shorn of its Western biological essentialism (see, for example, Weston 1991; Borneman 1992). One of these more instrumentalist views of kinship, which draws on Pierre Bourdieu's (1977; 1990) theory of practice, focuses on what kinship *does*, and on the uses to which it may be put, and is strongly based in ethnography (see Schweitzer 2000). Bourdieu's focus on practical kinship, however, tends to ignore the emotional qualities with which kinship relations are imbued (see Yan 2001; Peletz 2001). Others have subjected Schneider's contribution to a close critical scrutiny, and have sought to extend its range – theoretically, ethnographically, and imaginatively (see Bryant 2002; Faubion 2001; Franklin and McKinnon 2001b; Galvin 2001; Stone 2001).

I want to investigate how the apparently radical implications of the culturalist critique of kinship could reconfigure what some might see as its more mainstream and conventional antecedents (cf. Carsten 2000a). But this also involves attempting to bring together studies that have concentrated on kinship and knowledge practices in the West with those that have focused on non-Western cultures.

The architecture of this book reflects these aims. In the first half (Chapters 2–4), I concentrate on the "opening up," or revision, of kinship constituted by studies of gender, personhood, and the house. These chapters consider the potential of these tropes to refigure kinship in new ways, and the analytic implications that work on the house, gender, and personhood have for the study of kinship. In the second part of the book (Chapters 5–7), I focus particularly on the relation between "social" and "biological" aspects of kinship. I have noted that Schneider's distinction between nature and culture, and between "substance" and "code," was central to his understanding of how American kinship was constituted. The deployment of these terms in anthropological analysis has notably carried strong implications about the different nature of kinship in the West and "the rest." If Western kinship was marked by a strong separation between the order of nature and the order of law, the kinship of non-Westerners was often, by contrast, described as a domain for the mixing of nature and culture or the transformation of one into the other (see Carsten 1995a, 1997, 2000a; Latour 1993; Strathern 1992a; Weismantel 1995). But if it now appears that in a number of Western contexts these distinctions are not as clearly made as Schneider argued, then we may have to reexamine some anthropological certainties. In what ways do these forms of kinship pose a challenge to conventional anthropological definitions?

Anthropologists have been unavoidably confronted by the apparently rapidly changing imaginary space that kinship now occupies in the West. I began this chapter with a set of snapshots intended to capture just such a sense of innovation. Who could fail to be surprised by the idea of Orthodox rabbis debating the implications of the latest medical technology, or by an appeal, made on apparently common-sense grounds, to allow a posthumous conception to proceed? But of course such new imaginings have been at the heart of what anthropology has from the beginning brought to the social sciences. In the past it appeared that the myriad examples of how "they do things differently there" might promote new ways of understanding – and even perhaps new ways of doing – in the West. And this was nowhere more true than in the domains of gender, familial relations, and wider kinship arrangements. But the point of anthropology is not merely to come up with further examples of how particular people in particular places do things differently. It is also to engage in a more rigorous analytic project of comparison.

If the focus of the anthropological gaze has in recent years shifted to take in how "they do things differently *here*," then it is also time to put these new imaginary and experiential spaces to work in our analytic understandings of the comparative study of relatedness. In so doing, we might recall that the image of the stable and unchanging Western nuclear family that provided a buttress against an inhospitable world was just that – an image that only very briefly and partially ever conformed to reality.

The Chapters

I want to put all this – the everyday intimacy and the larger institutional arrangements, the foreign and the close-to-home, the apparent stability as well as the obvious dislocations and innovations – into the anthropological frame of how we study kinship. The vignettes with which I began this chapter capture some of these juxtapositions among the private emotional experiences, the public debate, and the legislative interventions in the world of kinship. One woman's search for her birth mother in Scotland; the complex attempts to resolve the contradictions between Jewish law and technological innovation in the modern nation state of Israel; Diane Blood's pursuit through the British courts of the "right" to have her husband's child – these stories highlight both the familiar and the new. They can be read as accounts of changing definitions of kinship, and of the interface between the supposedly private world of the family and the wider institutions in which it is embedded. All of these concerns are reflected in the chapters that follow.

I begin with the house. As I describe in Chapter 2, houses jumble up what anthropologists have been accustomed to separate. The close, lived intimacy of life inside houses, which often centers around the household hearth, involves feeding, sex, and economic arrangements. In the sometimes haphazard "side by sideness" of what happens in the house, we can begin to understand how ideas about bodies and about gender come to structure social relations. But houses are of course not just about warmth and intimacy, nor are they, in reality, static structures closed off from historical forces in the outside world. Colonial interventions in housing policies introduced new spatial and hygienic regimes. These underline the wider political significance of the rules and habits inculcated by and within house structures. The significance of houses lies not just in their "everydayness," whether familial or political. Houses also exercise a call on our imaginations and embody our personal histories. The memories of houses occupied in childhood may continue to exert a vivid emotional power (at once pleasant and disturbing) even when in adulthood we may be spatially as well as temporally dislocated from the houses we long ago ceased to inhabit. The power of these memories is likely to be all the greater when moving to a new house has been made necessary by external political upheaval. And this reinforces the connections between larger political processes and the supposed havens of family life.

I have already indicated that gender is implicated in the silent distinctions we make while carrying on everyday activities inside houses. And I have observed that the constitution of gender as a legitimate field of study within anthropology in the 1970s was part of that reformulation of the discipline in which the study of kinship lost ground. Chapter 3 focuses on gender and on the relation between gender and kinship. The discussion necessarily takes in the vexed relation between physical bodies and their cultural elaborations. If it seems impossible to move between kinship and gender without passing through bodies, then this suggests that the analytic separation of gender and sex might be worthy of further scrutiny. The distinction of gender from sex was originally conceived as a liberating device that could make possible understanding women's and men's variable roles without reverting to pregiven biological difference (see, for example, Ortner 1974; Rosaldo 1974; MacCormack and Strathern 1980; Rosaldo 1980; Ortner and Whitehead 1981). My aim, however, is not to suggest further analytic refinements or separations, or to contribute to the many arguments that have been made for the social construction of sexual difference. I suggest instead that by reintegrating gender, bodies, and kinship, we might find a way of *including* so-called biological processes as part of what anthropologists study when they study kinship.

In Chapter 4 I turn to anthropological studies of what constitutes a "person" – in terms of moral and spiritual qualities, and of connections to other persons. This theme, like gender, has been crucial to unpicking and reconstructing how anthropologists analyze kinship. I focus on a well-known dichotomy, proposed by many anthropologists since the 1970s, between Western bounded and autonomous individuals, and non-Western "relational" persons. The chapter is ethnographic as well as analytic, and it juxtaposes some familiar cases in the anthropological literature taken from Africa, China, and Melanesia with some less familiar material on posthumous births and on organ donation drawn from Britain and the United States. I suggest that the prominence of the individual in anthropological renditions of personhood in the West is in part the result of an undue emphasis on judicial, philosophical, and religious sources. It also reflects some unspoken assumptions about the relative insignificance of kinship in the West. If, however, we turn to Western contexts where relatedness comes to the fore and is strongly articulated (and these need not necessarily be the most obvious familial ones), then some rather less bounded and more relational ideas about the person are revealed.

Chapter 5 examines what anthropologists do when they engage in comparison, focusing on notions of bodily substance. This term has been used to analyze cultural perceptions of the properties of blood, milk, saliva, and sexual fluids and particularly their mutability and transformative potential. Like personhood, since the 1970s, "substance" has been a rather fruitful theme for analyzing how, in different cultures, people articulate and put into practice ideas about bodily transfers and physical connectedness. *Substance* has a very wide range of meanings in English, and these have been transferred into anthropology (often implicitly), where the term has been employed in several quite different ways. Examining how anthropologists have understood substance in the literature on North America, India, and Melanesia, I argue that this range of meanings is, strangely enough, one source of the analytic fruitfulness of analyzing relatedness through notions of bodily substance. Substance has been used by anthropologists to convey the mutable aspects of kinship. And this is because it carries the meaning of essence of a thing, its form, and its content, as well as its liquid properties. Kinship has often been taken to stand for what is given rather than what is made in its anthropological renditions, so that kinship studies have lacked a vocabulary for conveying change and fluidity in relationality. Partly because a focus on substance has highlighted the significance of bodily transfers and transformations, substance has itself come to stand for qualities of mutability in kinship.

Chapter 6 moves from ideas of physical connection to contexts in which kinship is said to come into being without procreative links. Here, once again, the theme of the biological and the social comes to the fore. Kinship may be demonstrated through the idiom of cofeeding, of living together, or of friendship. But what is the status of these kinds of kinship? Passing from an emphasis on cofeeding in Ecuador and Malaysia to assertions of kinship across ethnic boundaries in immigrant Southall in Britain and among gays in San Francisco who have been cut off from their birth families, I go on to examine narratives that I collected in Scotland about reunions between adults adopted in infancy and their birth kin. In the Western contexts, where we might most expect to find sharp distinctions between "social" and "biological" kinship, these boundaries often seem irrelevant, blurred, or difficult to ascertain.

In the final part of this chapter, I pursue the elusive boundary between physical and social connectedness further by focusing on metaphorical uses of kinship. In nationalist rhetoric, such metaphors come to exercise extraordinary emotional power over ordinary citizens. I suggest that part of the enticement of the metaphor of "nation as family" lies in the possibility that exists for slippage between metaphor and reality. In the context of warfare, not only can ties of kinship be drastically severed, but the threat or reality of acts of rape and resultant pregnancies and births create the possibility of a quite illicit and negative kind of kinship.

The interface between what is construed as "biological" and what is "social" is scrutinized through a different lens in Chapter 7. I have already noted that one major source for the recent revitalization of the anthropological study of kinship is the impact of reproductive technologies – on people's experiences of kinship, and on its public representations in the media. In Chapter 7 I examine some of the recent literature on this topic that suggests that advances in fertility treatments involve two simultaneous and apparently contradictory effects: a "technologization of nature" and a "naturalization of technology." It appears that these twin projects may have a dramatically destabilizing effect on Western notions of kinship, since kinship was a domain popularly conceived as resulting from ties based in nature and remaining outside technological intervention. Nature now appears to require the help of technology, while technology itself is said to be merely helping nature along a path it might have taken anyway (Strathern 1992a, 1992b; Franklin 1997). At issue here are the boundary between what is "natural" and what is "made" and the presumed natural basis of kinship.

Attending closely to scientific and academic discourse, it has been suggested that the new technologies may have a destabilizing effect not just on notions of kinship but on Western knowledge practices more generally. But what about actual experiences and practices of kinship? Are these really undergoing such profound change? Here the evidence is more equivocal. And this too is captured in the stories with which I began this chapter. When we look at the debates surrounding Diane Blood's efforts to change the HFEA rulings, or rabbinical discussions on the impact of reproductive technology, we are confronted by what is at once exotic and familiar. The most recent ethnographic accounts suggest both that people express their concerns about technological developments in familiar idioms – for example, in terms of incest or adultery – and that they may imagine them in quite new and sometimes unexpected ways.

TWO

Houses of Memory and Kinship

For many people, the memories of houses inhabited in childhood have an extraordinary evocative power. Perhaps this is attributable to the dense and myriad connections that link together what goes on in houses – processes of feeding and nurturance, the emotionally charged social relations of close kinship, and repetitive bodily practice through which many rules of social life are encoded – quite apart from their more practical, material, and aesthetic dimensions.

My own powerful "house memories" focus on a large kitchen table at which not only cooking and eating but also most family discussions, communal homework, and many games took place. This was the warm, at times overheated, hearth of a house, which combined, in curious ways, elements of an early twentieth century Central European, bourgeois, Jewish culture with the unconventionalities of left-wing bohemianism of the 1930s and of the postwar London intelligentsia. The house had a distinctly old-fashioned air, or at least an "out of time" quality, which no doubt partly resulted from my parents' uprooting from Nazi Germany and their subsequent dislike of change for its own sake. The enormous and often chilly "living room" was home to an ill-assorted collection of somewhat ponderous antique furniture and paintings. It presumably expressed rather accurately the tastes of a solid upper-middle-class home in 1920s Berlin. Needless to say, very little living actually took place there; this was a space reserved for special occasions and rather formal dinner parties.

There were, in reality, two foci to this house. One was the study-bedroom on the first floor, where my parents worked, read, and slept. In this book-lined room, warmed by the colors of bright kelim rugs, my parents would each night turn down a rather narrow divan, converting it into an apparently none-too-comfortable bed.[1] To the end, they adamantly rejected the suggestion of their busybody children that they might donate themselves, in what was after all a vast house, a specially dedicated bedroom with a proper bed. If the living room represented an earlier era of European bourgeois respectability, this study was its bohemian and intellectual antithesis. It made an emphatic and oppositional statement, in contrast to their own backgrounds and to the amazement of many visitors, about the marital and intellectual harmony and the values that were at the heart of my parents' lives and of the house they established together.

The other focus of that house was the large kitchen, situated on the ground floor, directly below the study, where most family living actually took place. This too held its surprises, remaining steadfastly unmodernized throughout the era of the fitted kitchen. Pride of place was held by an enormous cast-iron kitchen range, an original feature when the house was built but long out of use. Apart from its decorative value, the range provided storage space for a motley collection of tools and kitchen equipment – baking trays, pruning sheers, and, most memorably, a pair of truly Van Goghian gardening shoes. Other idiosyncratic features of the kitchen included a wall-mounted display box, which had indicated to servants of an earlier time the room in which a bell had been rung for their attention. At the large table in the center of the room, everyone had his or her place, just as they had their allotted role in the endless

---

[1] No doubt it is significant that the closest equivalent I have come across to this room is Sigmund Freud's study in the Freud Museum, nearby in Maresfield Gardens.

enactments of the family drama that characterizes such houses. The rituals of family meals were closely observed and central to the house. Timings were precise and not subject to negotiation. Visitors inevitably commented on the evening ritual of coffee-making, which took place at table in an old-fashioned Cona coffee-maker lit by a methylated spirit lamp. This operated on principles similar to a Victorian hourglass with the added application of heat. My father always ensured that the coffee was ready by the end of the meal, the Cona functioning rather like a measure of domestic time special to the house.

When I remember that kitchen, and the many arguments and discussions that took place over meals there, I always do so from the point of view of my customary seat at the table, visualizing other family members occupying their proper places too. Not surprisingly perhaps, as my brothers and I contemplate the gray procedure of dismantling the house following my father's death, it is clear that the study and the kitchen – the twin spiritual centers of that home – will be attacked last.

As the example of my parents' house suggests, for those who are later uprooted, the memories of houses occupied in childhood, or by previous generations, may be especially powerful. Dislocations in space may be erased by evocations of past practice that are given a stable location in the house. This formulation comes from Joelle Bahloul's (1996) evocative description of Dar-Refayil, a Jewish-Muslim house in Setif, in eastern Algeria, which reconstructs not just the relations of the author's maternal grandfather's family, but of a wider society too. From the 1930s to the early 1960s, this house was occupied by both Muslims and Jews. From Bahloul's intricate account of the space, its inhabitants, their everyday rituals of cooking and eating, their festivities, and their shared activities, we learn of a shared culture that continues to inhabit the memories of residents who still live there and of those now living in France. She writes, "The remembered house is a small-scale cosmology symbolically restoring the integrity of a shattered geography" (1996: 28). Bahloul emphasizes the importance of the spatial idiom and of the localization of activities in these memories.

Significantly, it is female memories, and shared domesticities that this description places in the foreground, for Dar-Refayil is above all the abode of women (1996: 30). As in the Kabyle case, which I discuss later in this chapter, divisions of space and activity cannot be extricated from distinctions of gender. But there is no doubt of the ability to evoke a wider culture from these small-scale activities. The disposition in space of the various families of the house – with the Jewish ones nearer the favored spot occupied by the landlord, and the Muslim families below – the organization of sleeping space, the different types of heating and cooking, the exchanges of special feast food, and the small services undertaken by Muslim women for Jewish women on the Sabbath – all bring into play the tensions and interdependencies of a complex, cosmopolitan, colonial culture. On the one hand, there was an emphasis on the "mixed-up" quality of social life, the communal and shared nature of the house. On the other, small separations and distinctions reflect the tensions and violence of colonial Algerian public life in the world outside the house, a world "framed by emphatic religions and ethnic distinctions" (1996: 46). Here anti-Semitism and racism on the part of the colonial Catholic population created a tripartite structure in which Jews were superior to Muslims, with whom they yet shared elements of domestic life, but were excluded from the Christian community (1996: 44–50). It is thus not surprising that domestic harmony between Jews and Muslims figures so largely in memories of the house they inhabited together, obscuring the differences that in the end disrupted their shared residence.

The Algerian example as well as the evocation of my own natal home in London make clear that memories of past houses are not just personally evocative, redolent of domestic kinship – indeed, they make kinship – but they also carry with them wider political significance. Houses may be symbolic loci of stability, but part of their power to evoke permanence must be understood in juxtaposition to the dislocations of history – a theme to which I return toward the end of this chapter.

Houses and Kinship

What goes on in houses necessarily does so in close juxtaposition. The house brings together spatial representations, everyday living, meals, cooking, and the sharing of resources with the often intimate relations of those who inhabit this shared space. It is the dense overlay of different experiential dimensions of living together in houses to which I want to draw attention. Rather than distinguishing different elements of what makes houses homelike, I suggest that the very qualitative density of experiences in the houses we inhabit leads many people around the world, including the Malays with whom I lived on the island of Langkawi, to assert that kinship is *made* in houses through the intimate sharing of space, food, and nurturance that goes on within domestic space. And because being "made" is usually opposed to being "given," houses are good places to start examining that theme.

But where does an anthropology of the house stand in relation to the anthropology of kinship? In the classic mid-twentieth century studies of British social anthropologists such as A. R. Radcliffe-Brown (1950), Edward Evans-Pritchard (1940; 1951), or Meyer Fortes (1949), houses hardly figure as the loci of kinship. This is because these anthropologists viewed the primary importance of kinship as providing a stable *political* structure in societies without state or governmental institutions. Kinship-based entities, such as the lineage or wider descent group, had a solidary function and gave continuity and stability to the political order. "Descent group theory" of this era thus focused on the sources of political cohesion in "societies without states" rather than on the minutiae of domestic life. What went on in houses was, by definition, likely to be of little interest. What was central to such studies was the form and structure of wider political groupings, which were recruited through kinship, and their sources of continuity. But in the more general intellectual shifts in social and cultural anthropology of the 1970s and 1980s, which I outlined in Chapter 1, from form to substance, and from structure to process, the way in which anthropologists studied kinship was transformed.

These intellectual shifts were fueled partly by the difficulty of applying "African models" of kinship to the societies of Melanesia and Polynesia to which anthropologists were turning their attention (see Barnes 1962). But perhaps more importantly, they also drew inspiration from a more historical reading of African and Asian societies that acknowledged the profound effects of colonialism and state power on contemporary political forms. A move away from seeing societies as locked in an "ethnographic present" and isolated from the effects of history and contact necessarily meant that kinship could no longer be considered simply as the source of the stable functioning of the political order. The anthropology of political processes increasingly involved the study of history and memory, of colonialism and the state, and of regimes of authority and control.

While mid-twentieth century kinship studies had on the whole concentrated on the role of men in maintaining the political order, feminist scholarship gave an impetus to studies that turned attention to the lives of women and to domestic processes. From the 1970s onward, the everyday significance of what went on in houses – domestic labor, child-rearing, the economy of the household – came increasingly under scrutiny. More processual understandings of kinship, which allowed for a greater experiential emphasis on the way kinship is *lived*, highlighted the importance of the house as a locus for everyday understandings and practices of kinship.

Although in retrospect one might characterize the shifts I have outlined here as occurring in a straightforward and linear fashion, in fact the transition from form to substance, and from structure to process, was not altogether smooth. In the anthropology of kinship of the 1970s and 1980s, we can also discern some characteristic returns to an older style in which a focus on structure and forms reasserted itself in new guises. And here too we shall see that the anthropology of the house had a role to play. But apart from recapitulating some of the recent history of kinship studies in anthropology, this chapter also has a more ethnographic aim.

I have asserted that for many people, kinship is made in and through houses, and houses *are* the social relations of those who inhabit them. The significance of what is created and learned in houses also takes us beyond the house. Here I want to draw attention to the shared understandings, bodily practices, and memories of those who have lived together. Houses are involved in the encoding and internalization of hierarchical principles that shape relations between those of different generation, age, or gender. And these valorizations have a significance beyond the intimate and everyday sphere of what happens in houses. They may be implicated in the way wider social distinctions in the polity or the state appear natural, given, and largely inescapable.

This chapter takes up some of these themes by looking at examples of what constitutes a house in Algeria, Madagascar, Malaysia, Poland, Colombia, Portugal, and Egypt. The examples are not intended to give a complete picture of the ethnography of the house, but rather to suggest that we may learn from the sometimes contingent and haphazard "side-by-sideness" of what goes on in houses. We may come to understand kinship in particular contexts through the things that people do and the everyday understandings that are involved in living together. And in this way, we may open doors to new ways of understanding everyday social relations.

Houses and Hearths

In many places, the symbolic focus of the house is the kitchen, the hearth, the place of cooking. The most important activities that go on in houses are those which emanate from there. Cooking and eating, the sharing of everyday meals, are in some ways the most obvious markers of what those who live together have in common. But important as these processes are in themselves, they gain an additional salience from their symbolic connotations and elaborations. In the Alto Minho region of northern Portugal, João de Pina-Cabral has described the hearth as "the sacred core of the peasant household" (1986: 39). Here the house, *casa*, is also known as *lar*, hearth or home, or as *fogo*, fireplace. What defines the household is the commensality of those who live under one roof. But the cooking fire also has strong purificatory powers, and fire plays a role in many household and village rituals. The souls of the dead are thought liable to follow any fire removed from the house where a dead person lies, and to be unable to find their way back. On the Eve of St. John's in June, fires are lit in every household yard, as well as in every hamlet and in the square of each parish. Jumping over these fires is a way of protecting households from evil but is also, of course, a source of entertainment and excitement. In childbirth, it is the household hearth that purifies the new baby by consuming the severed umbilical cord and thus detaching the baby from unclean, antisocial, prenatal influences. In all these and many other ways, we are told how the hearth symbolizes the unity of those who live together and endows this unity with sacred characteristics (Pina-Cabral 1986: 39–41).

The most sacred of all processes involving the house hearth in the Alto Minho region is the making of bread. Bread is food par excellence, the source of both physical and spiritual sustenance. It plays a special role in Christian symbolism, and this lends its production and consumption in the house a sacred aspect. Not surprisingly, bread-making is a particularly ritualized form of cooking. The receptacle for kneading and rising the dough, the *maciera*, must be kept ritually clean. Each household should produce its own bread, and the process is strongly linked to sexual reproduction. But this is reproduction without the impure connotations of sex. When a new household is established, the wife combines dough from her mother's house with freshly kneaded flour and water but with no yeast. After being marked with a cross, the dough is left to rise with either a small bottle of vinegar stuck in it or the trousers or hat of her husband next to it. The vinegar, which is described as rough or coarse, and the clothing are the male elements. In one of those moments where symbolism becomes almost unbearably explicit, if the dough does not rise, the male household head may himself be asked to sit on the lid of the *maciera*. Once it has risen, the dough is described as being "alive," and here the idea of bread-making as a purified expression of the biological reproduction of the married couple is quite transparent. Pina-Cabral demonstrates how bread-making is also symbolically linked to the conception of Christ. The household, its sustenance and reproduction, is associated via risen bread with the pregnancy of the Virgin Mary and with Christian myths of creation (1986: 41–5).

Some of these ideas and associations may seem familiar to European readers, but they are replicated in different forms in non-European contexts. In their ethnography of Colombia, Stephen Gudeman and Alberto Rivera (1990) show how the house underlies an indigenous model of the economy. Here food cooked in the household hearth is central in providing the "force" or "strength" of the workers of the house, enabling them to engage with the land and to produce the food that guarantees the viability and productivity of houses.

Strength is secured from the earth and used up as humans gather more. Control over this process is established through the house, for by using the resources of the house to sustain their work the people gain control over the results of their efforts (Gudeman and Rivera 1990: 30).

Not surprisingly, then, to maintain the house means simultaneously to physically keep up the dwelling and to feed its inhabitants. The house as physical entity is also a social and economic concern, and the metaphor of "economy-as-house" is powerful and pervasive in Colombia (1990: 40–1).

With these examples in mind, it is possible to read some classic examples from mid-twentieth century British social anthropology in a different light. Anthropologists today think of Evans-Pritchard's (1940) study, *The Nuer*, as epitomizing descent group theory as I outlined it in the previous section. But it seems that the Nuer thought of themselves not in terms of lineages, but of locality and shared residence. We are told that "[a] lineage is *thok mac,* the hearth, or *thok dwiel,* the entrance to the hut" (Evans-Pritchard 1940: 195). Apparently, Nuer informants often had difficulty in understanding Evans-Pritchard's enquiries about who belonged to what lineage (1940: 205). Gudeman and Rivera have commented on how different the history of kinship theory might have been if Evans-Pritchard had elaborated on the local imagery of hearth and home rather than importing the apparently alien corporation of descent group theory (Gudeman and Rivera 1990: 184).

The association of the material dwelling and its inhabitants, mediated by the hearth and by food cooked there, occurs very widely. In many parts of Southeast Asia, the medium through which houses and people are tied to each other, and to the soil, is rice. Among the Malay people with whom I carried out fieldwork in the early 1980s, rice is the prime source of nutrition and strength, and especially of healthy blood. The consumption of rice meals cooked in the hearth not only strengthens existing ties of kinship between household members, it can actually create such ties with those who have recently come to share residence, such as foster children or in-marrying affines. A fetus is said to be composed of the blood of the mother and the semen of the father. After birth, however, a child's blood is progressively formed through the consumption of food cooked in the house hearth. As the inhabitants live together in one house over time and eat meals together, their blood becomes progressively more similar – and this is especially true of the blood of brothers and sisters, which is said to be more alike than that of any other category of kin. I explore the gendered implications of these ideas in the following chapter, but the important point here is that shared meals and living in one house go together, and these two processes progressively create kinship even when those who live together are not linked by ties of sexual procreation. Not surprisingly, there is also a strong moral value ascribed to these processes: The motives of people who habitually go elsewhere to eat are likely to be viewed with suspicion. As I was repeatedly told, houses never have more than one hearth. A division of cooking and eating arrangements speaks of division between those who should be close – those who share a house. These points underline the way in which the house encompasses both material and symbolic aspects, and it is often difficult to extricate one from the other.

Thus hearths may frequently stand for the entire house, and eating together is often the most emphasized of social activities within the house. This clarifies that the links between material houses and the people who live in them, and the connections between those who live together, may be expressed in terms of eating and bodily substance. This is one way that houses, human bodies, and relatedness may be expressed. These are themes that I take up again in Chapter 5. But another theme that emerges from seeing houses through their hearths is the link between the house and marriage.

Houses and Marriage

Pina-Cabral's ethnography from northern Portugal makes explicit the way that the very establishment of a new house is linked to the procreative potential of its hearth in terms of the production of bread, and simultaneously to the reproductivity of the husband and wife who establish the house through the birth of children. Not surprisingly perhaps, the making of children and the making of bread are metaphorically linked.

That marriage is the central relation on which houses are based has been suggested by Claude Lévi-Strauss in his writings on what he terms "sociétés à maison," or house societies (Lévi-Strauss 1983, 1987). In his earlier work on kinship, Lévi-Strauss had emphasized the universal structural principles underlying different marriage systems. For Lévi-Strauss, it was marriage rather than descent that was central to the understanding of kinship. But in contrast to his British contemporaries, Lévi-Strauss was not particularly concerned with the functioning of social groups. In *The Elementary Stuctures of Kinship*, first published in French in 1949 and in English translation in 1969, the structural principles of exchange and reciprocity underlying different kinds of marriage systems were delineated in a form that was highly abstracted from the messy realities and the actual lived experience of kinship and marriage. Principles of exchange and reciprocity were, for Lévi-Strauss, manifestations of universal properties of human thought, which often expressed itself in the opposition of paired elements such as hot/cold, male/female, and above/below. These linked pairs of opposing terms were most obviously manifested in the structure of myths to which Lévi-Strauss turned his attention once it became clear that the underlying principles of kinship were always likely to be obscured by more contingent historical or demographic factors.

Lévi-Strauss's work on the house represents a quite radical departure from this structural stance in the sense that its starting point is a particular social institution, the "house," which is to be understood in its social and historical context. This is an attempt to delineate a specific type of society in which houses are not just socially significant, but take a particular social form – one to which existing categories of kinship analysis do not easily apply. European noble houses, for example, are named entities that possess ritual wealth as well as material estates. Through processes of inheritance and succession, these kinds of "houses" do not cease to exist when their members die, but are enduring social institutions perpetuated by both descent and marriage. Lévi-Strauss thus outlines a model of a "house society" that is positioned in an evolutionary frame. The house society is a kind of intermediary social form that occurs somewhere between societies that are regulated through kinship and those that operate through class.

In one way, we can thus see Lévi-Strauss's model as a departure from his earlier, much more abstracted and technical work on marriage systems. The notion of the house society has provided a fertile ground for ethnographers to explore (see Carsten and Hugh-Jones 1995; Joyce and Gillespie 2000; Macdonald 1987). Some of these more recent writings on the house have also suggested that in delineating the features of house societies as a distinct typology, Lévi-Strauss tended to fall back once again on a more rigid understanding of kinship, which in the end reverts to an emphasis on structure and form at the expense of content and process. Nevertheless, one attribute of houses as core institutions to which Lévi-Strauss seems to have pointed very accurately is their link to marriage, and this opens an avenue to explore the social processes in which houses are involved.

The link between marriage and the house is often materially expressed. Marriages are the occasion for house-building, renovation, or extension. The feasts that commonly celebrate marriage are often undertaken in a parental home, which must be suitably decked out for the occasion. In Columbia, Gudeman and Rivera describe how rites of passage are occasions of lavish public display, and are known as "throwing the house out of the window" (1990: 45). Malay marriage festivities also involve at least one, and preferably two, parental houses becoming public spaces of communal eating. Newly married couples here do not usually establish a new house until they have had one or more children. Instead, they live for a while with either the wife's or the husband's parents, and the parental house may be extended or partially rebuilt for the wedding.

A vivid expression of the link between marriage and the house is provided by the Zafimaniry of Madagascar. Maurice Bloch (1995) describes how, for the Zafimaniry, the gradual process of building a house and that of making a marriage are actually two sides of a single phenomenon. The process begins when a young couple make their previously secret liaison visible to their respective parents. This revelation is in fact a betrothal, and is followed by the groom constructing what is, for the time being, a rather flimsy and fragile new house. The house is established when its hearth is lit in a ritual manner, and for this to happen the new wife must provide the implements necessary for cooking. The hearth itself combines male and female elements, and once again the cooking process is an all too clear metaphor for sex. But houses, like marriages, are not really on stable foundations until the couple begin to have children. Fertility is the expression of a good marriage, but this is only gradually established. A wife returns to her parental home for the couple's first pregnancy (and even subsequent ones), and the groom must woo her back. As the couple gradually acquire children, the groom and his relatives strengthen and rebuild the house, substituting the soft, permeable bamboo with hard wood. The Zafimaniry speak of houses "acquiring bones" (1995: 78), and the image could hardly be more redolent of the corporeal quality of houses and their link to the bodies of the inhabitants they contain. Eventually, a successful marriage is made evident in many children, and in a hard, decorated, and beautiful house. In time, such houses become ritual sources of blessing, "holy houses," for their descendants.

This example, which brings together an aesthetic of the house with an aesthetic of the human relations within it, also underlines the processual nature of both house-building and of kin relations. The success of a marriage is made evident through time in the beauty of the house and the number and health of its children.

Houses, Bodies, and Persons

While marriage may be at the heart of the house, it is not its only relation. The Zafimaniry case also makes clear the strong association between a house and its children. Malays, like many other peoples, render this connection tangible by burying the placenta of a new baby, which is thought of as the baby's spirit sibling, in the grounds of the house compound. Houses and sets of children are physically connected.

Sets of children are strongly associated with the house, and each child also has a spirit essence, *semangat*, which itself is thought to be part of a sibling set. Because, for these Malays, groups of brothers and sisters are supposed to be the paradigm of kin harmony and morality, everything is done to safeguard their good relations. As they grow up in one house, then marry and have children, they move to different houses and cease to coreside. It is understood that after young men or women have established their own conjugal families, they will no longer put the interests of their brothers and sisters first. Quarrels are likely to come between siblings, and these are the most upsetting of all disputes precisely because siblings are so strongly enjoined to live in harmony. To prevent such quarrels, married siblings and their spouses are never supposed to live in one house together.

The residents of a Malay house often also include a foster child, who may have lived there since birth, or have arrived as a child or teenager. As in other societies in Southeast Asia, fostering is very common, and it includes both quite temporary living arrangements and those that are much more permanent. This lends a fundamental salience to the ideas about the capacity of food-sharing to create kinship among those not apparently related in "biological" terms, which I described earlier.

The importance of siblingship and fostering in the Malay case has wider implications for understanding kinship. I discussed in Chapter 1 how the anthropological literature on kinship has foregrounded ties between parents and children over relations between siblings, and how it has relied on a distinction between "biological" and "social" ties. The priority given to siblingship in the Malay case, together with the capacity offered by fostering and coresidence to transform ties with unrelated people into those of kinship, suggest ways in which we might question some of the assumptions of this kind of kinship analysis. In Chapter 6 I take up these themes again and explore the interface between "biological" and "nonbiological" ties more generally.

There are other implications to the material I have discussed so far. The Zafimaniry evocation of body imagery to describe the house is no isolated instance. In many parts of the world, the vitality of houses is expressed in terms of the human body or of an animating house spirit. One might think of this as reflecting the very close identification between houses and their people that has been noted from northern Portugal to the southern Sudan. The particular manifestation of body imagery or personhood in the house once again suggests links to kinship. In the Malay case, we have seen how the animation of both houses and people is expressed in terms of siblingship. In northwest Amazonia, Stephen Hugh-Jones has described how the Tukanoan longhouse, *maloca*, is sometimes talked of as a woman's body with a head, vagina, and womb (1995: 233). Here the house imagery focuses on gender and marriage. Each compartment of the *maloca* contains a married couple and their children. At ritual dances involving intermarrying *maloca* communities, affinally related households exchange food. In these rituals, the term "house" once again refers to both the physical structure and the people it contains. Visiting men present their affines with meat and fish produced by men; in return they are given large quantities of manioc beer, which has been brewed by women, as well as bread and meat cooked by women. As a couple living in a longhouse compartment have sons who grow up and marry, they will in turn build a house; their children's marriages establish new sets of affinal relations to be celebrated in similar feasts, and so, "like daughters of women who have become mothers in their turn, each compartment contains within it the germ of a future house" (1995: 233).

If houses seem often to serve as an appropriate metaphor for the bodies and persons they contain, they may also suggest that bodies and persons themselves cannot be divorced from wider notions of kinship. These are themes that I pursue in Chapters 3 and 4. But the close interplay between houses and the social relations enacted within them raises another set of questions that center on the issue of the social distinctions or values embedded in the way houses are laid out.

Social Distinctions of the House

In the Amazonian example I have cited, houses are divided into marked areas: The front of the house is more public and available to visitors, the rear more private and associated with its residents. There is a door reserved for men at the front of the house, one for women at the rear. The compartments of different brothers and their wives and children are marked off from each other, and arranged according to rules of seniority based on age. Certain spaces of the *maloca* are communal and shared, others are reserved for their close family occupants. Cooking is the province of women; with the exception of bread-making, which is done at a communal hearth, each individual family cooks in the relatively private space to the rear of the house. But meals, which combine male and female elements, are eaten by the *maloca* community together in a shared central space. Men usually eat before women and children (Hugh-Jones 1995: 228–31).

The Tukanoan *maloca* is by no means unusual in inscribing pervasive social distinctions of age and gender, insider and outsider, in a spatial idiom. The markers and boundaries within houses may be quite invisible to the uninitiated, but are no less absolute for that. Normally, of course, a local child internalizes the binding nature of social distinctions as she learns to negotiate her way around her own home space in a quite unarticulated manner. Stephen Hugh-Jones has vividly recalled his own young son's difficulties in learning to move about the *maloca* in an appropriate way, and the feelings of restriction, "like wearing a badly fitting suit of clothes," that accompanied this adjustment (Hugh-Jones: personal communication).

Perhaps the most well-known example of how gender distinctions are inscribed on the house space is Pierre Bourdieu's description of the Kabyle house in 1950s Algeria first published in 1970 (1990: 271–83). Bourdieu – acknowledging the pervasive influence of Lévi-Strauss on French anthropology of this era – later commented in *The Logic of Practice* that this was "perhaps the last work I wrote as a blissful structuralist" (1990: 9). This depiction of the house was an attempt to demonstrate the structural coherence of "practical logic." Bourdieu described the Kabyle house in terms of a series of oppositions between above and below, men and women, inside and outside, dark and light. The lower, dark part of the house was associated with women and animals. This was the site of intimacy and procreation, of sleep as well as death; it was used to store grain for sowing, as well as manure and wood. The light, upper part was associated with humans, especially men and guests, the fireplace, the loom, grain for consumption. This is where the "cultural activities" of cooking and weaving took place (1990: 273). The physical structure of the house reproduced the gendered divisions of the house space. The main beam was identified with the male household head; it rested on a main pillar identified with his wife (1990: 275).

While the Kabyle house could be described as a microcosm of the world, it also represented one half of the universe – the world of women, darkness, and domestic intimacy as opposed to the light, public world of men. The oppositions within the house were thus replicated as one stepped from inside the house to outside – from the world of women to the world of men. These oppositions now seem in some respects a rather static assemblage of meanings, although Bourdieu crucially makes clear how they are internalized through bodily movement, and how the paradigmatic movement of men is out of the house whereas that of women is toward the interior. The internal organization of space reverses its external orientation, "as if it had been obtained by a half-rotation on the axis of the front wall or the threshold" (1990: 281). Each external face of wall corresponds to an internal space that has a symmetrically opposed meaning:

The loom wall, which a man entering the house immediately faces on crossing the threshold, and which is lit directly by the morning sun, is the daylight of the inside (just as woman is the lamp of the inside), that is the east of the inside, symmetrical to the macrocosmic east from which it draws its borrowed light (1990: 281).

The threshold has a sacred significance due to the fact that "it is the place where the world is reversed" (1990: 282–3). The orientation of houses, however, is defined from the outside, and from the point of view of men – the movement is of a man stepping *out* into the social world. There is no doubt that inward movement is subordinate to outward. The house is a hierarchical world, and the fundamental hierarchy on which it is based is that between women and men (see Bourdieu 1990: 281–3).

If, as I have suggested, today Bourdieu's depiction of the house seems unfashionably structuralist, his later analysis (Bourdieu 1990) illuminates how apparently simple acts of negotiating a house space involve the internalization of hierarchy, and how it is the very unspoken quality of the correspondences between the social and spatial distinctions that makes them appear natural and unquestionable. His analysis thus provides a bridge between an earlier structuralism and a more phenomenological approach that pays more attention to how people experience living together in a house. We see how apparently neutral and insignificant acts such as washing clothes or eating a meal, and how apparently random placings within a house – where different household articles are stored, or who sits where at the table – are not just imbued with social meaning, they are crucially involved in the reproduction of meaning. When children learn how to behave properly in the house, they are internalizing social distinctions. Although this does not mean that such meanings can never be negotiated or challenged, we might surmise that it is harder to challenge what has never been said (see Bourdieu 1990; Toren 1990).

One important lesson to be learned from the house, then, is the significance of seemingly random and trivial observations (which a student on one of my courses once unflatteringly referred to as "the anthropology of brushing your teeth"). While what goes on in houses may appear all too familiar, there is no doubt of the important messages that these everyday activities convey. Nor is it surprising that thinking about the social significance of the house has also made a consideration of women and of children unavoidable. In many cultures, houses are the particular domain of women and of children; coming to understand kinship via the house thus has the effect of foregrounding them as subjects. Such a foregrounding, which began in the 1970s, was in many ways the beginning of an anthropology of gender. In Chapter 3 I pursue some of the links between the anthropology of gender and the anthropology of kinship.

Houses and History

The learning of social distinctions within the house is clearly not just a process with domestic significance; it has an inherently political import. The naturalization of hierarchy is thus one theme that connects domestic kinship to the world outside the house. Although much work remains to be done on these connections, houses are inevitably part of wider historical processes, linking domestic kinship with other political and economic structures. At the beginning of this chapter, I referred to the apparently nostalgic memories that the former occupants of Da-Refayil keep of their shared residence. It is clear that, far from constituting a kind of safe haven isolated from the world, as we sometimes like to imagine, the house and domestic families are directly impinged upon by the forces of the state. However harmonious the social relations of Da-Refayil remain in the memories of its erstwhile residents, these relations were irrevocably disrupted by the colonial context and the Algerian war of independence.

In a similar manner, the apparently rather romantic meanings of the Zafimaniry house that I described are placed in sharp relief by Bloch's moving depiction of their French colonial setting – this time, Madagascar. In the aftermath of an anticolonial revolt in 1947, in which rebels attacked urban centers by passing through Zafimaniry territory, the French burned down the Zafimaniry village where Bloch later worked and attempted to send the inhabitants to concentration camps. Most of the villagers went into hiding in the forest, and their persistent reluctance to return can be explained not only by their fears, but by the fact that the French had destroyed the holy houses of the village, disrupting the flow of blessings from the ancestors and making it clear that the villagers had failed in their obligations to these ancestors. It was only by ritually repairing the original marriage, the source of blessing to the descendants, that the village could eventually be rebuilt and once again inhabited, and the flow of relations restored (Bloch 1995: 69–70, 82–3).

It is perhaps not surprising that in many colonial contexts the task of imposing a "modern" order should focus on housing. In keeping with recent anthropological writing on the political processes of colonialism and the state, Nicholas Thomas (1994: 105–6) has written of the way "colonial projects" involve an attempt at a total social transformation that may itself be resisted by the colonized. Even where the colonized express resistance as an adherence to old forms, however, he suggests that the new terms in which such resistance is expressed are themselves part of a "whole transformative endeavour." In Fiji, as elsewhere, housing and sanitation were the subject of much transformative attention from colonial officials in the late nineteenth and early twentieth centuries. Official reports emphasized the aim of social advancement of native society through reform and regulation. Meticulously detailed written regulations governing how and where houses could be built, where rubbish or animals could be kept, and how many people could occupy a house apparently had as their object the improvement of hygiene and sanitation. In this respect, results were inconclusive (1994: 118–19), but Thomas demonstrates how legislation did crucially affect the visibility and accessibility of rural housing to the colonial state. It was of course no accident that control over housing, and the imposition of a "modern" – that is, European – standard of order should increase the possibilities of the state conducting surveillance over the local population, as well as restricting and controlling the population's movement. Thomas describes how in Fiji, native society was to be bettered but kept distinct from its European counterpart, and the aim of preserving village life was in part to be achieved through the codification of local custom – which thereby became in many respects enshrined and inflexible. In fact, such legislation, while congruent with a policy of cultural separatism, had much to do with control over labor and with keeping the indigenous population out of the plantation sector, which was reserved for imported indentured Indian workers (1994: 105–42).

In nineteenth century Egypt, the colonial regime made a similar attempt to control and modernize the rural population to ensure agricultural production. Timothy Mitchell (1988) uses the term *enframing* to convey a Foucauldian sense of the disciplinary power that the colonial order sought to impose on the rural population. Housing was central in the imposition of a system of frameworks that was to infiltrate, re-order, and colonize, but above all to place the local inhabitants under the surveillance of an all-seeing state (1988: 35). The village population was to be fixed in place and monitored in its daily tasks. Resistance to an op-pressive regime of disciplinary measures was apparently countered in the 1840s by the imposition of a system of model villages under the control of local landowners. The model housing designed by French engineers "divided up and contained" space, specifying its precise dimensions and abstracting it from the people and activities that went on in the house. Mitchell likens this modern housing to barracks or schools in their en-framing capacity. Space was ordered rather than chaotic; houses could be planned, standardized, and read like a text, and were subject to statis-tical report (1988 42–8). Mitchell contrasts this model housing with an indigenous form he sees as exemplified by Bourdieu's description of the Kabyle house. The organization of space in the Kabyle house, according to Mitchell, can be thought of

. . . as attentiveness to the world's fertility or potential fullness. Such potential or force plays as the rhythm of life, a life not made up of inert objects to be ordered, but of demands to be attended to and respected, according to the contradictory ways in which they touch and affect each other, or work in harmony and opposition, or resemble and oppose one another (1988: 51).

Unlike its modern counterpart, the Kabyle house does not enframe; it provides no place from which the individual can observe, it provides no fixed boundary between interior and exterior, and "it is not an object or a container but a charged process, an inseparable part of a life that grows, flourishes, decays and is reborn" (1988: 53). The juxtaposition of the Kabyle house to the model houses of French engineers opens up serious questions. Leaving aside the rather romanticized gloss given to

Bourdieu's description (a gloss that passes over the hierarchical inscriptions of the Kabyle house) and the geographic and temporal leap that assumes a parallel between nineteenth century Egypt and twentieth century Kabylia, we are told nothing about how local inhabitants received the Egyptian model houses, or how widespread was their imposition. However meticulous the specifications of engineers, they imply nothing about how closely plans were adhered to, or the proportion of housing to which they were applied. To judge from contemporary Egypt, this project had limited application and/or success. In neither the Fijian nor the Egyptian cases do we learn nearly as much about the indigenous reception of colonial ideas and plans as about the ideas and plans themselves. Here there is a need for a more intimate historical anthropology to complement the emphasis on colonial discipline.

Nevertheless, the connections between the house and the political processes of the state make it clear that the meanings with which houses are invested are not simply a source of stability. These meanings are themselves enmeshed in historical processes. They may be used as a resource to represent the unchanging past and resist a "modernizing" state project, or they may be harnessed as a vehicle for change. For a more nuanced account of the interplay between the "heavy hand of the state" and local practices, I turn to Frances Pine's (1996) contemporary description of the shifting relation between the house and the state in the Gorale region of southwest Poland. Here villagers are known by their house name, and houses are a prime source of personal and familial identity just as they are in the Alto Minho region of Portugal. It is significant, however, that only local people are aware of these house names. In their dealings with officialdom, villagers use surnames imposed by the state and church (Pine 1999: 51). As in the Portuguese case, there is a strong link between the house and marriage, and houses are also sources of spiritual and physical well-being (Pine 1996: 446–7).

Pine describes how houses in the Gorale are closely associated with all major rituals, and they are themselves enduring entities that persist through mechanisms of succession and inheritance. We may thus see them as sources of the kind of stability that has already been delineated in the Algerian or Malagasy cases. But Pine also links the centrality of the house, as an institution, to the economic and political marginality of the Gorale, its geographic remoteness, and its exclusion from the state from the late nineteenth to mid-twentieth centuries (1996: 454; 1999: 48–51). In the face of a long history of relentless poverty, the Gorale villagers' relations with the outside world turned on trade, migrant labor, marketing, banditry, and smuggling. The two naming systems to which I alluded previously are thus a reflection of a deep split between what Pine refers to as an "inside" and an "outside" system (1999: 51). In their dealings with each other, Gorale villagers behave, as she puts it, like "proper peasants"; that is, they strongly adhere to a collective morality that centers on hard work and industry. But when they enter the outside world as migrant laborers, entrepreneurs, or traders, they shift to an alternative set of values that emphasizes cunning, entrepreneurial skill, and individualism. Pine likens this kind of "trickster behaviour" more to values associated with groups such as Gypsies in Eastern Europe than to those often ascribed to more sedentary peasants (1999: 45–8).

One interesting feature of this case is the way that, in the face of attempts at incorporation by the socialist state in Poland in the 1960s and 1970s, the house retained its centrality as a social institution. While the state took over many of the functions of the house in terms of child-rearing, health care, and education, it was also perceived as a threat in terms of collectivization and the destruction of the family farm. Under these circumstances, villagers materially embellished and elaborated their houses, continuing to find in them a prime source not only of identity, but also of resistance to an oppressive state. Houses also provided a kind of mask that disguised and legitimated activities associated with the informal economy. Although in practical terms the importance of houses may have diminished, their ritual significance increased (Pine 1996: 454–6; 1999: 53–5).

With the collapse of socialism, however, houses and their land became, as they had been in the presocialist era, a major practical resource in terms of subsistence. The state nevertheless continues to be perceived in negative terms, reinforcing the divide between the autonomy and individualism with which Gorale villagers deal with the outside world, and an internal world in which expressions of local identity, such as houses, are ever more elaborated (Pine 1999: 57–9). Thus under conditions of profound socioeconomic and political change, the house was in some respects a buttress of stability and provided an idiom of resistance, but its very endurance also revealed a capacity to adapt and to incorporate and generate new practices and meanings.

The Meanings of Kinship

Why begin a book on new kinship with an exploration of the house? The answer I hope is obvious: because for many people all the different processes involved in living in houses, taken together, make kinship. I have concentrated on houses as a way of underlining the varied local meanings that kinship encapsulates as well as a key to understanding its practical everyday significance. Hearths are obvious sources of physical sustenance, but they are also often the symbolic focus of the house, loaded with the imagery of the commensal unity of close kin. Houses are material shelters as well as ritual centers. Their very everydayness both suggests the importance of what goes on within their walls and also makes it liable to be dismissed as familiar and mundane. When we focus on this familiarity, we can see how the divisions of the house are simultaneously inscribed by often unarticulated social distinctions. In moving about the house, residents learn, embody, and convey differences of age, gender, and seniority. We have seen how houses provide anchors of stability. They can be havens in both a literal and metaphorical sense, the stuff of harmonious memories, but in part through their wider links with the economy and polity, they can also be fragile, vulnerable to attack and disruption.

I find it impossible to understand what a house is divorced from the people and relations within it. Houses offer us a way of grasping the significance of kinship "from the inside," that is, through an exploration of the everyday intimacies that occur there. This allows a suspension of some preconceptions about the formal characteristics of kinship in analytical terms so that we can begin from first principles to unravel the particular significance of kinship in local contexts.

The prioritization of local understandings should not, however, be taken to imply that an understanding of the cultural workings of kinship simply amounts to a description of cultural particularities, and thus precludes generalization or comparison. In the chapters that follow, I place in comparative perspective some of the issues or problems that have emerged from recent explorations of the meanings of kinship in local context. Discussions of personhood, gender, notions of substance, biological and social kinship, and the effects of reproductive technologies may be used to grapple with the problem of what kinship is in the local sense, and also allow us to examine critically what it is anthropologists do when they analyze kinship.

THREE

Gender, Bodies, and Kinship

The Hungarian Vlach Gypsies studied by Michael Stewart (1997) view men's and women's bodies as fundamentally different from each other. Their differences result from the polluting consequences of sexuality, which mean that women's bodies are potentially dangerous, and for this reason the separation between their lower and upper bodies must be symbolically marked. Women's lower bodies are covered by several layers of clothing, and cleanliness of the body is always rigidly marked off from processes of cooking and eating.

Among the Malay Muslims whom I studied on the island of Langkawi, women's behavior is often strikingly assertive, and women and men interact in many everyday contexts in a relaxed manner. And yet in more formal contexts, and at certain stages of their lives, quite strict rules of sex segregation apply. In a somewhat confusing way, these Malays seem to assert that men's and women's bodies are quite similar, but also appear in other ways to think of these bodies as quite different from each other.

In southern India, an old anthropological chestnut, Dravidian kinship, has recently been reanalyzed in terms of gendered similarity and gendered difference. Cecilia Busby (1997a, 2000) suggests that, rather than dividing the world simply into two, in terms of which relatives one may marry and which one may not, Dravidian kinship is fundamentally based on a radical distinction of relatedness that occurs between those of the same sex and between those of opposite sex.

All of these examples (which I consider in more detail later in this chapter) combine attention to kinship with material on gender. In this chapter, I look at the anthropological study of gender, which since the 1970s, in many respects, eclipsed the study of kinship. In its concern with domestic relations, the household and its economy, the symbolism of procreation, and ritual transformations of women and men, the study of gender apparently took over a similar space to that of kinship in the anthropological imagination.

And yet one might argue that the fields of gender and kinship had been inextricably intertwined since the very beginning of kinship studies in anthropology. Johan Bachofen's (1861) theories about "primitive matriarchy" and Lewis Henry Morgan's (1877) comparative study of the evolution of institutions of marriage, technology, and property holding, which were taken up by Freiderich Engels in his *Origins of the Family, Private Property and the State* (1884), both involved a complex interweaving of theories about the evolution of family forms and political institutions in which kinship and gender were inextricably linked. One strand of later feminist studies, in fact, shows very obvious links to some of the early work in this field. Although I do not consider their relationship in detail here, studies of the political economy of kinship and gender, and on the related institutions of marriage and property (see, for example, Young, Wolkowitz, and McCullagh 1981; Meillassoux 1981; Peletz 1995a), can be traced back to these earlier pioneering works.

Kinship studies in the mid-twentieth century, too, could hardly isolate kinship from gender. Claude Lévi-Strauss's (1969) theories of marriage alliance, to take one example, had at their core, as later feminists pointed out, a theory about relations between men and women that involved men exchanging women in marriage. One reason that kinship and gender could not be dissolved into separate fields of study was pointed out by Sylvia Yanagisako and Jane Collier (1987) as part of the feminist critique of kinship: They were both based on the same indigenous Western theories of biological reproduction. David Schneider's study of *American Kinship* (1980) had an enormous impact on later feminist theories of gender precisely because it illuminated biology as a native cultural system in the West. It thus enabled feminist scholarship to show that the way in which men's and women's bodies, or sexual procreation, were conceived could not simply be taken for granted as "natural" or given. Kinship and gender as analytic fields in the West rested on similar assumptions and indigenous theories, which had to be dismantled or "denaturalized" in order to advance understandings of gender crossculturally. However, Schneider's work failed to provide any standpoints that could be used to show how different people might have different understandings or practices of kinship with any given cultural system – and why this would be significant (see Yanagisako and Delaney 1995).

In this chapter, I focus on what the study of gender does for the study of kinship. Part of the answer to this question is that paying attention to distinctions of gender places some of the classic subject matter of kinship studies in a different light. The study of gender played a crucial role in the gradual shift in attention in anthropology from the functioning of social institutions to the symbolic construction of persons and relations. Inevitably, gender raised questions about power and social control, and the processes through which such control is reproduced.

In asking, what does the study of gender do for the study of kinship, I also argue that it is time to bring kinship back into gender. Gender without kinship tends to become trapped in a rather abstract and arid set of questions that arise from the way gender itself is constructed as an analytic model. The analysis of gender rests on an explicit separation of the "natural" from the "social," or the given and the made. Schneider (1984) showed that a similar separation was implicitly present in the study of kinship. A starting premise for the study of gender is that we need to be careful to distinguish the apparently natural differences between men and women from the cultural meanings that are attached to them. And yet it is striking that the question of what is given and what is made is not one we ask with the same persistence or anxiety in other contexts – for example, when examining birth or death crossculturally.

Bringing kinship and gender back together, I suggest, is a way to reintroduce the relational and dynamic into a realm of theorizing that tends to become trapped in a circular set of arguments. It allows us, in other words, to escape the terms in which debates about gender have been set while still drawing on the powerful insights that the study of gender relations has made possible. But before I attempt this redrawing of anthropological boundaries, it may be helpful to cover a little history.

The Anthropology of Gender

When we think about gender relations, we necessarily consider what goes on in houses and what anthropologists have often referred to as the "domestic sphere." How is the labor of women and men differentiated in particular cultural contexts? What are the meanings and symbolic associations attached to this division of labor? These are some of the first questions that anthropologists interested in gender relations have asked. But studies of gender have also led anthropologists to question any simplistic or universal definition of what constitutes "the domestic" and to look carefully at the underlying assumptions on which an analytic distinction between the "political" and the "domestic" is based. In the same way in which we saw that houses (which might be thought of as quintessentially domestic spaces) have myriad links to the polities of which they are part, anthropologists have also used the study of gender to refigure an overdetermined opposition between the domestic and the political spheres.

So, there is a strong and obvious connection between the analysis of gender relations and the study of the house as a means of opening up discussions of kinship. I shall return to this connection at various points in this chapter. The appropriation of topics like procreation or the domestic economy as legitimate subjects for the study of gender rather than kinship marked a more general shift away from kinship in the 1970s and 1980s. As the focus of anthropological studies switched from the institutional functioning of society to processes of symbolic construction of persons and relations, kinship began to lose ground, and gender was one of several areas that replaced it. The shift from kinship to gender was also a direct reflection of the rise of feminism inside and outside the academy (see, for example, Moore 1988; Schneider and Handler 1995: 193–8).

Feminism gave an impetus to studies of gender by highlighting the importance of variation in the roles played by men and women, and perceptions of these roles, in non-Western cultures. Many feminist scholars clearly hoped to find evidence of societies where relations between women and men were on a more equal, or at least a radically different, footing from those in Western societies. Studies of the relation between sexual hierarchy and property clearly had such an aim in view – particularly in societies where property was of rather little significance, and therefore relations between women and men might be egalitarian in spirit (see, for example, Leacock 1978; Sacks 1979; Etienne and Leacock 1980; Collier and Rosaldo 1981). And this was a means to constructing a political argument about the noninevitability of Western social institutions and the possibility of changing them.

The separation of gender, as social role, from sex, as the material body, distinguished the physical differences in the bodies of men and women from the cultural meanings ascribed to them. This provided a key to explanations of female subordination, which tended to return to the physical characteristics of women's and men's bodies (see Ortner 1974; Rosaldo 1974). By demonstrating that whatever these physical attributes were, the cultural perception of physical bodies was neither inevitable nor predictable, anthropologists could move toward a more open, and less predetermined, account of relations between women and men (see Rubin 1975; MacCormack and Strathern 1980; Rosaldo 1980; Ortner and Whitehead 1981; Moore 1988). Such accounts were in tune not just with feminist aspirations to provide a nondeterminist understanding of relations between the sexes, but also with a more general relativist spirit in anthropology.

In the space of a few years, however, the liberating distinction of sex from gender seemed to lead to something of a theoretical impasse, and this can be traced to the very separation on which the anthropological study of gender was based.

Sex and Gender

I suggested that the division between sex and gender rested upon a prior distinction between biology and culture, which was also implicit in the study of kinship but which had a peculiarly overdetermining effect on gender as a topic of anthropological enquiry. How did this come about? Although the distinction between sex and gender initially appeared to offer an escape from physical determinism, as a theoretical device it also represented a rather uneasy compromise. Anthropological studies of the 1980s focused on cultural variation in the way gender was constructed. Paradoxically, however, a problem emerged with the "unmarked" term: sex. Although it was possible to document how in different cultures the bodies of men and women, and relations between them, were understood in quite different ways, this did not resolve the question of the analytic significance of the actual physical attributes of the body. This was the problem to which the anthropology of gender always seemed to return. And various writers confronted it in different ways.

In their important critique, Yanagisako and Collier (1987) argued that, in both the analysis of gender and of kinship, anthropologists had taken for granted what had to be explained. They had assumed the existence of natural differences between women and men when they should have sought to explain how such differences were conceived:

Rather than taking for granted that "male" and "female" are two natural categories of human beings whose relations are everywhere structured by their difference, we ask whether this is indeed the case in every society we study, and, if so, what specific social and cultural processes cause men and women to appear different from each other (Yanagisako and Collier 1987: 15).

The powerful argument of Yanagisako and Collier was that both the study of kinship and of gender had been defined by Western folk concepts of biological reproduction. Rather than constituting two separate fields, they were in fact united in their basis in the same set of naturalistic assumptions (see Yanagisako and Collier 1987: 31–2).

As Yanagisako and Collier acknowledged, their argument was very strongly influenced by Schneider. Drawing a parallel with his *A Critique of the Study of Kinship* (1984), they suggested that, like kinship, gender could not be separated from the "biological facts" that defined it (1987: 33). The solution they proposed, once again influenced by Schneider, was a dismantling of the discrete analytic domains that had defined the study of kinship and gender, and a focus instead on the generation of cultural meanings. An important part of Yanagisako and Collier's analysis was the outright rejection of any precultural, material givens. It was thus logical that they should also propose a rejection of the dichotomy between "material relationships and meanings" and between sex and gender (1987: 42).

Here it is important to distinguish two steps in Yanagisako and Collier's argument. The first is the rejection of a separation between culture and biology. Like Schneider, they convincingly demonstrate that this separation has been at the heart of the anthropological analysis of both kinship and gender. Because it is so grounded in particular Western folk models of biology – models that they argue do not universally hold – it is untenable. The second step they take is to suggest that there simply is no precultural biology outside social construction. This part of their argument seems to me more problematic, partly because, as others have pointed out, the idea of social construction itself apparently depends on something "out there" to construct (see Moore 1994: 18). In other words, this part of their argument seems to rest on the very distinction it is seeking to demolish. The second difficulty, which is connected to the first, is the continuing sense of unease about what has happened to the material body.

One attempt to refine Yanagisako and Collier's argument about the social construction of the meaning of gender is Shelly Errington's (1990) discussion of sex, gender, and power in Southeast Asia. Errington's argument focuses on indigenous notions of power, on personhood, and on the meanings ascribed to the body. She suggests that "human bodies and the cultures in which they grow cannot be separated conceptually without seriously misconstruing the nature of each" (1990: 14). In order to analyze the culturally specific set of meanings attributed to bodies and sexual difference in the West, Errington distinguishes "Sex," "sex," and "gender." By "Sex" she denotes the particular construction of meanings given to the body in the West, the "gender system of the West," while "sex" refers to human bodies in general. "Gender" is "what different cultures make of sex" (1990: 26–7).

In some respects, it is clear why Errington is led to make this further distinction. As she sees it, Yanagisako and Collier conflate "sex," as a general feature of human bodies, with "Sex," the particular meanings given to these bodies in the West (1990: 28). It is because Yanagisako and Collier see sex as inextricably bound up with Western cultural construction that they advocate abandoning the dichotomy and seeing everything as cultural construction. Errington points to the problems this entails – specifically, to what does gender refer if not to the physical body?

The problems of sex and gender are equally recalcitrant in approaches that take a more extreme constructionist position than that of Errington. Such approaches, influenced by the work of Michel Foucault (1978), show how sex is the product of historically and culturally situated discourses. They rest, to varying degrees, on the idea of discourse as central to producing both sex and gender as ontological realities (see Busby 2000: 11–16). Thomas Laqueur (1990) has described how Western understandings of the anatomy of sexed bodies have radically altered from the time of the ancient Greeks to the twentieth century. With the help of contemporary anatomical drawings, he shows that sometime during the eighteenth century, a remarkable shift occurred from a hierarchical one-sex model of human anatomy, in which male and female sexual organs were perceived as essentially similar, inside-out versions of each other, to an incommensurable two-sex model, where male and female bodies were seen as radically different. Here then is a specific example of the way sex is constrained by particular historical and social contexts.

Although Laqueur considerably destabilizes the relation between biology and culture, and between sex and gender, he remains careful to maintain "a distinction between the body and the body as discursively constituted, between seeing and seeing-as" (1990: 15). Interestingly, he suggests that the reasons for not abandoning this distinction are, in the end, ethical and political.

The allowance for some kind of residual domain for "prediscursive bodies" that both Laqueur and Errington make is not, as I understand it, present in Judith Butler's (1990, 1993) writings. This more radically constructionist model dissolves the distinction between sex and gender; both are mutually constituted through the repeated enactment of appropriate gender performance. While this position is apparently a logical one to take, it inevitably raises certain questions:

How stable and how fundamental is gender identity? What is the implicit status of gender that certain rites can only produce what already exists? Has the dissolution between sex and gender permitted gender to simply replace biology as destiny? Can we avoid such recourse to teleology? (Morris 1995: 578).

If the determinism of sex seems to have been replaced by the determinism of gender, it is paradoxical that bodies should still be on the agenda at all. Yet they figure largely (if somewhat abstractly) in Butler's follow-up to *Gender Trouble* (1990), entitled *Bodies That Matter* (1993), in which she seeks "to explain in which way the 'materiality' of sex is forcibly produced" (1993: xi). In this version:

Construction not only takes place in time, but is itself a temporal process which operates through a reiteration of norms; sex is both produced and destabilised in the course of this reiteration. As a sedimented effect of a reiterative or ritual practice, sex acquires its naturalized effects . . . (1993: 10).

This is a sophisticated rendition of a performative position, the central point being that the very act of referring to bodies actually helps to create them. As Busby (2000: 11–15) notes in her important critique, however, Butler's notion of performance is quite removed from actual everyday practice, and is grounded in linguistic and philosophical theory. In this sense, it appears rather remote from the kinds of everyday activities observed by anthropologists, as well as from either Foucault's own understanding of the materiality of the body (see Busby 2000: fn. 7, pp. 233–4) or his analysis of particular historical institutions and contexts.

In various renditions, we can see how the terms of the debate about sex and gender always refer back to a seemingly inescapable distinction between biology and culture. The strength of the constructionist position lies in the way it acknowledges the "problem" of the apparent givenness of sex. The difficulty with the proposed solution is that it is too encompassing. The determinism of the physical facts has been replaced by the impossibility of escaping "discursive reiterations." But more generally, we can see how the endless tacking between sex and gender has constrained discussion to a rather abstract and arid set of questions that seem to preclude setting the terms of the debate differently. For the moment, then, let us set this discussion to one side, and look at a particular example.

Gender among Hungarian Gypsies

At the beginning of this chapter, I pointed out the connections between an anthropology of the house and the anthropology of gender. Houses might be an obvious place to begin to look at how distinctions of gender are inculcated, lived, and reproduced. Among the Hungarian Vlach Gypsies, or Rom, studied by Michael Stewart in the mid-1980s (Stewart 1997), notions of bodily cleanliness and pollution are strictly enforced. These ideas are strongly gendered, and they have a spatial dimension. Although the bodily functions of both men and women are shame-inducing, it is women, above all, whose bodies carry the polluting consequences of sexuality, which must be kept under control (Stewart 1997: 204–31). This is reflected in women's clothing. Once they begin to menstruate, women should keep their heads covered by a headscarf, and their lower bodies are dressed in a long skirt covered by an apron. In the house, the potential dangers of bodily pollution are kept at bay by a rigid separation of operations that involve cooking and those concerning bodily cleanliness. Stewart vividly describes the horrified reaction of a woman whose washing machine was broken when he attempted to empty it using the nearest water jug at hand (Stewart 1997: 207). The bowls and water used for washing kitchen utensils must not be mixed with those for washing persons or clothes. Dishes are left to drain rather than being dried with a towel. In a nice juxtaposition of two sets of ideas about purity and pollution, Stewart wryly observes how Gypsy friends appropriated his own dish towels as foot rags (1997: 207).

The furtive separation of activities that involve bodily cleanliness and a rigid division between the upper and lower bodies of women are two of the most obvious markers of the way in which ideas about cleanliness and pollution are deeply embedded in Gypsy practices and modes of thought. It is clear that Rom women are far more the bearers of bodily pollution than men, and that the source of this is thought to lie in processes of menstruation and childbirth. These are not subjects that are necessarily spoken about, but the symbolic meanings are inculcated and reproduced through ideas about the moral consequences of being unclean, and are made manifest in the foul smells of bodies and houses, as well as in skin blemishes and infertility. Of course, the symbolic connotations of these ideas are neither restricted to the body nor to domestic space. Just as we saw in the last chapter how the house is very far from an isolated haven from the outside world, Stewart makes clear how the gendered meanings of Gypsy bodies and domestic cleanliness have a powerful political dimension. This reflects relations between Gypsies and non-Gypsies, or *gaźo*.

While it might be thought that, as in many other cultures, the shameful connotations of Gypsy women's bodies would lead to their seclusion in order to protect their modesty, this is far from being the case. In fact, Stewart describes how, in addition to being responsible for household cleanliness and keeping pigs, women are not only scavengers in the local town, but also intercede in many of the dealings that the Gypsies have with the state bureaucracy. As has been observed for Gypsies in other contexts (see, for example, Okely 1983), the upper/lower or inner/outer body division is also "about" ethnic relations between the Rom and the *gaźo*, whom the Rom perceive to be deeply unclean: "As the clean Rom was to the dirty *gaźo*, so the upper/inner was to the lower/outer body" (Stewart 1997: 229).

But Stewart also demonstrates that the shameful and polluting connotations of the female body reflect the particular experience of Hungarian Rom in the postwar communist state and the pressure they were under to assimilate into mainstream society as factory workers and proper citizens. While Gypsy women were to some extent a buttress between Gypsy men and the outside world, men created an ideal and transcendent world in brotherhood and song, insulating themselves from state values of productive labor by making money through sharp dealing of horses on the market. Here the aim was a rapid turnover, a quick deal, that demonstrated Gypsy superiority over the *gaźo* in cunning and intelligence. The alternative moral universe of the Gypsies involved living out a life free from the natural – and polluting – consequences both of sexual reproduction (carried and contained in the bodies of women) and of the production values strongly inculcated by the communist state.

The example of the Rom is one where the bodies of men and women are sharply differentiated, and where these differences have consequences outside the body for clothing and rules about cleanliness. But we can also begin to see how the differences between men and women have a complex political dimension involving dynamics of power and control among the Rom themselves, and involving their relations with the outside world. Here it is clear that the activities that go on in houses, or rules about bodily cleanliness, are not just constitutive of a "domestic" order. They are part of a larger worldview that is specifically Rom.

Sameness and Difference

Of course, it is not always the case that men's and women's bodies, or the activities in which they engage, are seen as radically opposed. In the Austronesian world, for example, it is common for *similarity* between men and women to be stressed rather more than the *differences* between them. Here the unmarkedness of gender often extends to ideas about the body. In a striking example of this, Jane Atkinson (1990) has vividly described how, among the Wana of Sulawesi, men are thought to menstruate, get pregnant, and give birth in the same way as (if rather less efficiently than) women. This perhaps might be thought to be a rather extreme case, but it underlines the point that an anthropology of gender needs to be concerned not just with the construction and valorization of difference but also with similarity. And this, I shall argue, necessarily involves thinking about gender in terms of kinship.

One of the strengths of Yanagisako and Collier's argument, to which I alluded earlier, was their suggestion that rather than taking sexual difference for granted, we should examine how it is understood in different cultures. By critically examining difference, they argued, we would unite the domains of gender and kinship. Building on Yanagisako and Collier's insights, as well as other discussions of the constructionist position, Henrietta Moore (1993, 1994) has drawn attention to the problems of privileging sexual difference over other forms of difference – for example, those of race or class – as well as over similarity. Ascribing to sexual difference an ontological priority not only hierarchizes forms of difference, but leads to an exclusion of race and class, thereby constituting a realm of "pure gender," isolated from other idioms of differentiation.[1]

Moore notes how Western assumptions about binary sexual difference *between* men's and women's bodies are challenged by cases where differences are understood to exist *within* the bodies of women and men. For example, Marilyn Strathern's (1988) depiction of gender differences in Melanesia, which are internal to both male and female bodies and are ascribed to different parts or substances of the body, makes the distinction between sex and gender rather difficult to locate. Here persons are composite and androgenous. Gender, Strathern argues, is elicited in relations with others. And rather than persons having a unitary gender identity, what is being elicited from persons depends on whether these relations are between those of the same sex or those of a different sex. Sexual difference "must be made apparent, drawn out of what men and women do" (Strathern 1988: 184). In such contexts, Moore suggests, "it is unclear exactly what gender as a concept or category refers to" (Moore 1994: 14). But Strathern's argument, that gender in Melanesia refers both to "the internal relations between parts of persons, as well as to their externalisation as relations between persons" (Strathern 1988: 185), makes clear that we are being presented with a radically different model from the one on which the Western distinction between sex and gender is conventionally based.

---

[1] See Stolcke (1993) for an illuminating discussion of the naturalization of inequality in class society. She suggests a homology as well as an ideological link between the way that ethnicity (as a social or cultural distinction) derives from the supposedly natural differences of race, and the way gender derives from the apparent natural dimorphism of sex. In both cases, social inequalities are legitimized by ascribing to them a natural foundation. Significantly, Stolcke pursues her analysis not through a constructivist argument but by emphasizing the historical specificity of these naturalizing maneuvers.

Like Moore, Signe Howell and Marit Melhuus (1993) have subjected the notion of difference to critical examination and drawn attention to the importance of analyzing conceptions of sameness alongside those of difference. Long before this, Gayle Rubin had pointed out that although men and women are different, "they are closer to each other than either is to anything else – for instance, mountains, kangaroos or coconut palms" (1975: 179). Rubin suggested that exclusive gender categories were in fact based on "the suppression of natural similarities" (1975: 180). Drawing on these arguments, I want to step back from the distinction between sex and gender, and to examine notions of difference and sameness in the particular context of Malay kinship.

Like many other Southeast Asian cultures, Malays do not particularly stress gender difference. In many contexts, Malays instead emphasize the similarity between men and women (see Atkinson 1990; Errington 1990; Karim 1992, 1995; Peletz 1995b, 1996). Malay kinship can be thought of as being a process of gradually creating similarity between people and abolishing difference to an outside realm (see Carsten 1997). In this way, the Malay material can provide a counterpoint to the discussion so far. It can be used to scrutinize the significance of valuing gendered sameness rather than difference. Above all, the Malay case shows how ideas about gender refer not just to static and fixed *categories* but can be understood much more clearly when placed in the dynamic and *relational* context of kinship.

Women and Men in Langkawi

For the Malays with whom I lived in the early 1980s, gender is not necessarily the most salient way of differentiating people. And the degree to which it does matter is always dependent upon the age of those involved. This fits with a broader pattern found elsewhere in the region (see van Esterik 1982; Brenner 1995; Karim 1995a, 1995b; Ong and Peletz 1995). Sex segregation and women's seclusion do occur, as in many other Muslim cultures, but to varying degrees, depending on age and marital status. At the time of my fieldwork, gender difference was most marked in the years immediately prior to marriage. Even in these years, the degree of segregation and seclusion was quite limited. And while men's authority was related to their ability to earn a living, and this usually declined in old age, women's authority continued to rise as long as they were in possession of their full mental faculties.

In childhood and old age, gender difference tended to be relatively insignificant, while in the years around marriage it was rather more marked. It was very striking, however, that there were certain "moments" when gender difference did seem to be particularly stressed. These moments occurred around rituals of the life cycle: birth, circumcision, marriage, and death.[2]

In Langkawi, at the birth of a baby boy, the Muslim call to prayer is sounded. This is not the case when a baby girl is born, and is one of the few ways in which gender difference is marked at birth. Malays in Langkawi and elsewhere always emphasize their desire to have children of both sexes. A couple with one or more sons will want to have a daughter, and those with daughters will want a son. As elsewhere in Malaysia, girls are thought more likely to look after parents in their old age and are desired partly for this reason (see, for example, Peletz 1996: 220).

While early childhood was a time when boys and girls associated in a relaxed manner, the ritual of circumcision quite clearly distinguished girls from boys. At the end of the period of ritual taboos that follows childbirth, the midwife made a small incision to the clitoris of a baby girl (see Laderman 1983: 206–7). This rite was part of the final stage of the birth rites, which were small-scale and intimate, and usually did not involve feasting or guests in the way that male circumcision did. By contrast,

---

[2] I would emphasize that all these rituals are Islamic ones, and gender differentiation is a prominent theme in many Islamic cultures. But just how Islam is locally elaborated is, of course, highly variable (see, for example, Bowen 1993; Lambek 1993), as is the way gender is elaborated within Islam (cf. Peletz 1995b, 1996).

male circumcision was a large-scale ritual, usually involving several boys from one locality. At the time of my fieldwork, boys were circumcised at about the age of ten, but in the more distant past, circumcision seems to have been regarded as necessary for marriage and the assumption of sexual relations. In the 1980s, male circumcision marked the beginning of the period when young men and women were most strongly separated and differentiated. This separation was an important feature of betrothal rituals, during which the bride and groom were not supposed to see each other at all.

If gender differentiation was at its height in the period just prior to marriage, marriage itself began the gradual lessening of these restrictions. From late middle-age onward, the differences between men and women were rather unmarked. In these years, women tended to behave in a strikingly assertive and often jocular manner toward men. Death rituals once again brought gender differentiation to the fore. The ritual preparation of male and female corpses undertaken by men or women, respectively, vividly marked the difference between men and women in various ways (one being that women are always buried in their white prayer robes). Birth, circumcision, marriage, and death rituals express gender differentiation both through the appearance and behavior of the principal participants, and in the way that attendance at these rituals was very strictly sex-segregated; this was in marked contrast to most nonritualized contexts of daily life in Langkawi.

There is also a sense in which women and men in Langkawi were distinguished in terms of ideas about their bodily substance. Mothers are seen as the source of a child's blood, and having blood in common is thought to make the bond between a mother and her children particularly close. The blood of a father is thought to be "a little different" (*lain sikit*). But there are also various ways in which male and female bodily substance can be said to merge. This is also expressed in the ideas about blood. After birth, a child's blood is formed through the consumption of food cooked in the house hearth. Both breast milk, a quintessentially "female" substance, and semen, a quintessentially "male" substance, are perceived as forms of blood.

In the process of a couple living together in one house over time, eating meals together, and having children, the blood of a husband and wife is thought to become progressively more similar. Conversely, at the time of their birth, the blood of a group of brothers and sisters is thought to be more alike than that of any other category of kin. By analogy, however, as brothers and sisters grow up, marry, and move to separate houses, their blood is thought to become progressively more different. The two processes of progressively becoming similar and progressively becoming differentiated, in which eating together in houses is central, reflect the two idioms of gendered difference and similarity that I have sketched.

It was quite clear at the time of my fieldwork that the house in many respects constituted a female domain. It was where women spent most of their time while men were occupied with the outside world – in migrant labor, fishing, the coffee shop, or the mosque. However, any notion of bounded gendered domains was also quite problematic in the context of the fluidity of notions of gender that I have described. Part of the social significance of the house is that it is at once domestic and private, and simultaneously a public and political unit. The public world of the community involves not just men but men and women. The responsibilities that villagers see as central to communal life – such as visits to the sick and dying, and arranging and attending marriage feasts – apply to women and men equally, particularly as married couples.

In these Malay ideas, we can see how gender articulates notions of difference *and* of sameness. One might say that it is both categorical and fluid. In some contexts, bodily substance is gendered: semen and bone can be associated with men, blood, flesh, and milk with women. But there is also a sense in which blood itself transforms, and is subject to transformation. Blood is what kin have in common, but it is mutable. The convertibility of bodily substance means that the extent to which either bodily substance or relations between kin are inherently gendered is quite weak. To some extent, and in some contexts, we can speak of gendered bodily substance or gendered relations, but there always seems to be a possibility of merging these gendered contrasts, or blurring the distinctions between them. What is crucial here is that these dynamic and transformative processes involve the making and unmaking of kinship. To consider gender without kinship would not only make very little sense in this context, it would omit the crucial relational dynamics involved in both kinship and gender.

Gender and Kinship – a Classic Case

So far, I have argued that in order to understand notions of gender in a fully relational and dynamic form, we need to place them in the context of ideas and practices of kinship. This argument of course rests on the assumption that gender and kinship are inextricably linked. And it might just as well be put the other way around. The idea that understandings of gender underlie kinship was a crucial part of the move away from kinship in the anthropology of the 1980s, which I described at the beginning of this chapter. I now want to turn to a recent example, which demonstrates the fruitfulness of reexamining, through the lens of gender, a classic case in the anthropological literature of kinship. This time the example comes from South Asia.

Busby (1997a, 1997b, 2000) has subjected the complexities of Dravidian kinship terminology in South India to an elegant reanalysis that hinges on gender, and on the inextricable connections between gender, personhood, and kinship. Dravidian kinship terminology is well known in the anthropological literature for making a fundamental distinction between "parallel" relatives and "cross" relatives. Parallel relatives are those descended from two siblings of the same sex – either a pair of brothers or a pair of sisters. Thus two parallel cousins are the respective children of two brothers or two sisters. Cross-relatives are those descended from siblings of different sex – a brother and a sister. Cross-cousins are the respective children of a brother and a sister.

Anthropologists have long been intrigued by a central feature of Dravidian kinship, which is that the distinction between cross- and parallel cousins also distinguishes those whom one may marry from those whom one may not. This occurs through the kinship terms themselves. Thus the term for one's cross-cousin of the opposite sex actually *means* "husband" or "wife." The terms for parallel cousins, conversely, connote siblingship rather than marriageability. The distinctions of Dravidian kinship terminology thus have the effect of dividing an individual's social universe into two kinds of kin: those whom one may marry, and those who are like siblings and whom one may therefore not marry.

This kind of terminological distinction raises important questions for anthropologists. The most fundamental of these is about the relationship between language and culture. In one view, the terminology itself determines how individuals perceive their social world and therefore how they act. It is because Dravidian terminology (a feature of language) divides the world between marriageable and nonmarriageable kin that people act in the appropriate way. In this view, language is prior to behavior – it determines how we see our world and how we act. But one could also argue that such a system suggests that behavior comes prior to language – and this is because, when someone marries the "wrong" person, he or she still uses the appropriate kin term for his or her spouse. This follows from the fact that the term for spouse inescapably carries the meaning of "cross-cousin." When one marries someone who is not a cross-cousin, the appropriate terminology is adopted.

Anthropologists of South Asia have seen Dravidian kinship terminology as an expression of a particular "alliance structure" – a set of rules governing marriage between kin, which occurs systematically over generations. This kind of analysis tends to emphasize the abstracted features of a particular kind of kinship system. But Busby suggests that the analysis omits the crucial experiential aspect of how it *feels* to be actually immersed in this kind of social world. For this reason, she draws attention to the connections between kinship, gender, and the person. She argues that the distinction between cross- and parallel relatives, which is fundamental to a Dravidian system, is based on a radical distinction between same-sex relatedness and opposite-sex relatedness (1997a: 38). Here men pass on male substance in the form of semen, and women pass on female substance in the form of blood and breast milk. It is for this reason that women are thought to be more closely related to their mothers, and men to their fathers. "A woman passes on her femaleness to her daughters, and a man passes on his maleness to his sons" (1997a: 37). This means that what links a woman to her children is different from what links a man to his, and therefore the children of a brother and sister "are as little related to each other as they could be: they are in fact potential spouses" (1997a: 38).

It is because bodies are conceived as inherently gendered that a very firm distinction is made between cross-cousins (that is, a mother's brother's child or a father's sister's child) and parallel cousins (a father's brother's child or a mother's sister's child). Parallel cousins are related through a same-sex link and are considered like brother and sister, and thus as too close to marry. Cross-cousins, related through a different-sex link, are inherently marriageable.

While there is something satisfying about the simplicity of Busby's exposition, it also leaves some unanswered questions. These focus on issues of sameness and difference. For example, if gender difference is categorical, fixed, and inherent to the body, it is not immediately clear why a father's sister's child should be exactly equivalent to a mother's brother's child. One might expect differences between them. And one might also expect it to matter whether the child in question is a son or a daughter. For example, a father's sister passes on her femaleness to her daughter with whom she has a same-sex link. But apparently less of this female substance is transferred to her son, with whom she has an opposite-sex link (see Busby 1987b: 264). Yet in terms of the categories of Dravidian kinship, both the son and daughter are cross-cousins to an individual to the same degree. This suggests that these categories cannot be reduced to understandings about gendered bodies in a very straightforward way.

Nor is it entirely obvious what it is about cross-cousins that makes them suitable marriage partners. Busby concentrates on the issue of gendered difference of cross-cousins. But presumably there is also an equally complex issue of gendered similarity at work, since one could connect to someone different by marrying a nonrelative. What is it about cross-cousins that makes them related to the precise degree that is appropriate for marriage?

Here we see how there is nothing totally predictable in the way gendered difference or similarity is understood. Clearly, gender is part of the distinctions that are made in a Dravidian system, but it is also apparent that some kinds of gender distinctions matter more than others, or matter in a different way. Put simply, it is difficult to abstract gender out as a single principle from the other salient idioms of differentiation that are being made. And this complicates Busby's argument that Dravidian categories rest on fundamental distinctions of gender that "emerge as distinctions of the body and bodily substance, distinctions in the way that substance can be passed on to children" (1997a: 40). It would seem that there are various gradations of sameness and difference, conceived in terms of kinship and gender together, that have implications for marriageabilty.

Reconstituting Gender, Bodies, and Kinship

I want to return now to the questions with which I began this chapter, and to ask whether we can put some of the examples I have discussed to work in getting beyond the analytic impasse to which the division between sex and gender apparently leads. Earlier on, I drew attention to a sense of unease that remains when we simply do away with "preconstructed" biology. That same unease is underlined in other recent discussions of gender in anthropology. For example, Jane Atkinson (1996) has highlighted the problematic implications of her constructionist depiction of Wana beliefs about the similarity of men's and women's bodies to which I referred earlier (Atkinson 1990). Her unease centers on how this description ignored important facts about the high mortality rates of Wana women in childbirth. And this recalls Laqueur's point about the ethical and political reasons for maintaining some kind of hold on biology.

A similar dissatisfaction lies behind Rita Astuti's (1998) reconsideration of her own earlier readings of gender, kinship, and personhood among the Vezo of Madagascar (Astuti 1993, 1995a, 1995b). The Vezo, like many other Austronesian people, can be said to emphasize the acquisition of characteristics that shape the person through life rather than innate qualities. To a considerable extent, Vezo emphasize that their identity is fluid and processual, derived from the environment rather than being inborn. In some respects, such ideas also hold for gender, as Astuti has shown. But in a recent article, she describes her surprise at the extent to which the sex of a child matters to the Vezo at birth. Exploring the reasons for this, she argues that the dichotomy between sex and gender is one aspect of a fundamental division between essentialist and nonessentialist understandings, which are probably a universal cultural phenomenon. Rather than pursue a constructionist position, she therefore suggests that we should retain the analytic opposition between sex and gender, which at least to some extent reflects indigenous Vezo ideas (Astuti 1998).

I find Astuti's argument about a universal disposition to make a distinction between attributes that are seen as innate and those that are acquired persuasive. But I also think the danger in using terms like "sex" and "gender" is that we may make assumptions about how, and at what points, such distinctions are made in different cultures, and thus obscure their differences and similarities.[3] The problem can be illustrated by the

---

[3] Astuti acknowledges that "There is no doubt that 'sex' and 'gender' are analytical categories that would make no sense to my Vezo friends" (1998: 46). But she argues that the difference between what anthropologists see as biologically given and what

Vezo ethnography. Astuti describes what would happen if she asked Vezo women what they meant by saying a child was either a boy or a girl at birth; they would respond in terms of the baby's sexual organs. In other respects, boys and girls are said to be just the same at birth, and will have to learn to behave in the appropriate ways for their gender.

The only difference occurs at the moment of birth, when boys appear facing downwards, and girls appear facing upwards. This is because boys must avoid looking up their mother's vagina, which will be taboo (*faly*) when they grow older; but girls have none of these problems, since mothers and daughters are made in the same way (*sambility iaby*, they all have the same vagina). As they come into the world, boys and girls behave in a manner appropriate to their gender, *and they do so as a matter of fact, although nobody quite knows how it actually happens!* (Astuti 1998: 40, italics in final sentence added).

Astuti argues that Vezo view sex as "a categorically fixed and 'intractable' trait of the person" (1998: 41), in contrast to gender, which is processual and acquired. But I am intrigued by the apparently fixed and intractable way that boy and girl babies know the appropriate, gendered way to behave at the very moment of birth. Is this particular bit of behavior an aspect of sex, gender, or both? These questions underline the fact that the distinction between sex and gender may not be as clearly demarcated as might be assumed, and that the distinction itself will be made in a manner and at points that are culturally specific.

The point that we do not know in advance how difference or sameness will be construed, or what will be regarded as innate or acquired, is also beautifully captured in Astuti's earlier ethnography (1995a). This demonstrates how the Vezo make a very consistent (and Malagasy) opposition between the fluidity and movement of personhood in life, and the fixed and unchangeable nature of people in death. As Astuti makes clear, for

is culturally constructed is "not so remote" from the difference Vezo see between what is fixed and intractable – that is, being born with a penis or a vagina – and the negotiable and processual aspects of becoming a man or woman (1998: 46–7).

the Vezo, an "unresolved tension" (1998: 5) exists between what is fixed and what is alterable in human identity, and this is well expressed by their fraught relations with the dead. Thus, to a very considerable extent, death, rather than birth, is the repository for ideas about what is fixed and unalterable in human identity.

It seems inherently plausible that people everywhere would be unlikely to make a distinction between culture and biology in exactly the same place and in the same manner. In my description of Malay notions of gender, I made constant recourse to ideas and practices of kinship. These indicate a considerable blurring of distinctions between what we would refer to as "biological" phenomena and their "social" attributes. When people are said to become kin through living and eating together, it is difficult to know whether this should be considered as a "social" or a "biological" process. It seems to me that it is important to grasp it as both: Bodily transformations entail social obligations, and vice versa. Indeed, it is not very clear just where the boundaries between biological and social attributes would lie.

This has implications for the argument about sex and gender. The kinds of distinctions that are made, or not made, in Langkawi between women and men mix together elements of bodily function with "social" attributes – "sex" and "gender." Rather than taking idioms of difference and sameness for granted, I have considered them in the wider context of Malay ideas about relatedness, recognizing that this is an appropriate domain for the expression of such distinctions.

Conclusion

The argument of this chapter has been very simple. I have suggested that "gender," "kinship," and the "person" are all different ways of looking at a similar set of issues. Both gender and the person were instrumental in the reconfiguration of the anthropological study of kinship that took place in the 1980s. And this is a theme I continue to explore in the following chapter, which focuses on the anthropological study of personhood. Placing gender in the context of kinship has the virtue of reintroducing the relational and dynamic into a realm of theory that otherwise tends to become trapped in a quite abstract and static set of oppositions.

In the process of recontextualizing gender in kinship, I have attempted to unsettle some of the separations upon which the anthropology of gender has been constructed. I have proposed to bring together, rather than to separate, sex and gender. It seems to me that this separation, although apparently useful, results in a tendency to reify both categories. It thus constrains discussion about gender to a somewhat teleological search for prior causes. And it also assumes we know where that distinction will be made. Something recognizably like this distinction may well be made in different ways in different cultures. Rather than doing away with biology, I suggest bringing together sex and gender as a way of retaining biology as part of what anthropologists have to understand. Atkinson's reminder about the significance of maternal mortality to which I referred earlier is salutary here.

I have underlined the importance of understanding ideas about gender in the wider context of practices and notions of relatedness. Conceived in its broadest sense, relatedness (or kinship) is simply about the ways in which people create similarity or difference between themselves and others. Those between women and men are inextricably linked to other kinds of relatedness. But we need also to remember that neither gender nor kinship is a thing in itself. Neither can simply be isolated from other markers of social difference or inequality, such as those of class or race. Nor can either be abstracted from the historical contexts in which such differences are made salient – as is demonstrated in the recent studies of Laqueur (1990), Peletz (1996), Stolcke (1993), and others. If anthropology aims to understand the terms in which people perceive and create difference and sameness in other human beings, we should recognize that kinship, in the fullest sense of the term, is one good way to begin.

FOUR

The Person

Diane Blood's protracted litigation in Britain to establish her claim to undergo artificial insemination using the sperm of her deceased husband, and Anna's long search in Scotland to make a connection to a birth mother from whom she had been separated since babyhood, are very much contemporary Western stories. These vignettes with which I began this book both apparently speak to very topical issues at the heart of how the person is perceived.

It seems of obvious significance that such stories can be framed around the importance of knowledge about genetic connection, or in terms of the "rights" of individual human beings. But I shall show in this chapter that it is also possible to read these stories in a different way, as illuminating how close kin ties are intrinsic to the social constitution of persons. The obviousness of this observation, which has long been central to anthropological analyses of how the person is constituted in many non-Western contexts, has been obscured by the assumption that kinship is of much more marginal significance in Western capitalist societies. So, this chapter sets out to do two kinds of work: to delineate some of the complexity, and the different sources, of Western ideas about the person, and also to trace the history of anthropological understandings of personhood crossculturally. Upsetting a rather oversimplified dichotomy between a Western individualized person and a non-Western "joined-up" person makes clear the centrality of locally and historically specific practices and discourses of relatedness.

In an interview published in 1997, Marilyn Strathern suggested that the study of personhood – what it means to be a social agent in different historical and cultural contexts – was one element that played a crucial role in revitalizing kinship studies in the 1980s. "The concept of the person," she suggested, "appeared to present a key to describing the connection between relationships on the one hand, and values on the other, which was almost tantamount to the same configuration that the notion of society itself offered" (Strathern 1997: 7–8). The study of personhood brought together what had previously been "distributed in different ways." It could not avoid analyzing how persons were formed – procreation and reproduction – and the relations in which persons were embedded. In this way, it forced a reconsideration of what kinship itself meant, and "provided a new focus of critique" (1997: 8).

The examples that I cite in this chapter amply demonstrate how notions of the person draw upon procreation beliefs, the implications of being close kin, ideas about the body, and spiritual and moral aspects of the self. Personhood also provides links to the concepts of house and gender that I have considered in previous chapters, and to the notions of substance that I analyze in Chapter 5. A focus on personhood not only brings together different aspects of sociality, it can also help unlock the way anthropologists have analyzed indigenous notions of relatedness. But this underlines how if personhood has been a means to critique kinship, it may itself be due for a makeover. It also suggests that we can use kinship to critique the study of the person.

Two Types of Person

Strathern's depiction of the significance of the anthropology of the person at a particular moment in anthropological history suggests that personhood was both a continuation of certain classic themes in anthropology – for example, procreation, kinship relations, and property – but it also allowed the introduction of new perspectives, in which local meanings would be foregrounded. The former of these two strands drew some of its inspiration from Marcel Mauss and Meyer Fortes, while the latter has been more obviously influenced by the work of David Schneider and Clifford Geertz.

Mauss's essay on the person, delivered as a Huxley Memorial Lecture to the Royal Anthropological Institute in 1938 (and reprinted in a collection edited by Carrithers, Collins, and Lukes in 1985), stands out because he touches on all of this. In tracing a development in the category of the self, beginning with the Pueblo Indians and culminating with modern European society, Mauss demonstrates how understandings of personhood are formed in a particular historical and cultural context, and he shows the connections of these ideas to institutions of kinship and property. His aim is to demonstrate that, far from being self-evident or natural, the concept of the person has, as he puts it, a "social history" (1985: 3). Concepts of the person differ along with "systems of law, religion, customs, social structures and mentality" (1985: 3). Anthropologists today, however, would want to shed the evolutionary assumptions he made.

Mauss shows how, in the case of the Pueblo Indians, the clan is made up of a number of persons, but here the person is encapsulated by the social role *(personnage)*, and "the role of all of them is really to act out, each insofar as it concerns him, the prefigured totality of the life of the clan" (1985: 5). Personhood, in other words, could not be separated from clanship, and was not a vehicle for individual conscience. In ancient Rome, however, Mauss argues, the social role was abstracted as a legal concept, and the citizen was invested with rights and duties as a legal person. To this juridicial notion of the person, Greek philosophers added a moral meaning: The person became the bearer of a moral conscience. With Christianity, this "moral person" was invested with metaphysical qualities, and this notion of the person as bearer of individual consciousness, and as a fundamental category to which thought and action applied, was further developed in modern European philosophy. Thus:

> ... from a simple masquerade to the mask, from a "role" *(personnage)* to a person *(personne)*, to a name, to an individual; from the latter to a being possessing metaphysical and moral value; from a moral consciousness to a sacred being; from the latter to a fundamental form of thought and action – the course is accomplished (1985: 22).

Mauss's argument has an evolutionary cast, and it is significant, given the historical moment at which the lecture was delivered, that he clearly perceived the "moral strength" (1985: 22) of the concept of the person to be under threat in the Europe of the late 1930s. For personhood is defined in Mauss's essay principally in legal and moral terms, as an abstract and theoretical concept, and investigated largely through legal history and philosophy.

This leaning toward a philosophical and legal understanding of person-hood is echoed in later studies, particularly the works of Louis Dumont (1980, 1985) and the collection edited by Carrithers, Collins, and Lukes (1985) in which Mauss's essay is reprinted. Dumont makes no secret of his allegiance to Mauss: "Faithfulness to Mauss' profound inspiration seems increasingly to be a condition of success in our studies, his teaching the cardinal organizing principle of our research" (Dumont 1980: xlvi). Dumont's study of caste in India, *Homo Hierarchicus* (1980), is conceived as a comparative work in the French sociological tradition. Not only has "caste something to teach us about ourselves" (1980: 1), but it is precisely because "Indian society ... is so different from our own" (1980: 2) that the comparison may be particularly revealing. The contrast is in terms of "fundamental social principles": Whereas "traditional" Indian society is founded on hierarchy, the ideology of the "modern" West is founded on equality (1980: 2–4). This has profound implications for concepts of the person. For while in the modern societies of the West the value of the individual, as bearer of a unique and equally valued identity, has reached its supreme expression – indeed, the individual is conceived as "quasi-sacred" (1980: 4) – in India, the notion of the person is subsumed to the hierarchical ordering of caste groups to which each person belongs. Thus while traditional society is characterized by "holism" and based on "a collective idea of man" (1980: 8), modern society is suffused by individualism: Society is thought of as made up of a collection of equal individuals.

What is significant for my purposes here is that Dumont sets up a contrast in the strongest possible terms. On the one hand, there is modern society, in which:

... the Human Being is regarded as the indivisible, "elementary" man, both as a biological being and a thinking subject. Each particular man in a sense incarnates the whole of mankind (1980: 9).

On the other, there is traditional society, which emphasizes the collectivity, with each person having a particular place in a hierarchical order.

Such a sharp contrast in notions of the person between the "traditional" and the "modern," or the "West" and the "other," as is sketched in the work of Mauss and Dumont, has perhaps a certain rhetorical value, but it is also potentially misleading. It is precisely because these authors draw so heavily on legal history, philosophy, and theology in their accounts of the West – domains in which there is no doubting the process of circumscribing the individual as a legal and religious entity at a particular historical moment – that we are given a rather rarified view of what constitutes the person in Western contexts. In the non-Western examples, by contrast, it is not law or philosophy that is at issue but contexts in which a collective ideology comes to the fore – most notably, caste or kinship.

In the remainder of this chapter, I ask whether we can upset this dichotomy between the Western bounded and autonomous individual and the non-Western "joined-up" person. Can we find aspects of nonbounded and less individualistic personhood in the West? Are there less holistic, more individualistic notions of the person even in societies that place great emphasis on the collectivity? In seeking to destabilize this contrast, I also want to pay close attention to sources and contexts – to the particular domains from which we draw our descriptions, and how these color our conclusions, and to the process of domaining itself (cf. Yanagisako and Delaney 1995).

The Non-Western Joined-Up Person

The obvious place to look for notions of the person that emphasize connectedness, or nonindividuality, might be in the kind of lineage-based societies that are organized around descent from a common ancestor, which I referred to in Chapter 2. Here wider kin groupings have a strong collective identity. Even in these cases, however, we shall see that there is a space for the expression of more individualized notions of the person – although the particular form they take is not necessarily predictable.

Meyer Fortes's ethnography of Tallensi personhood (1961, 1983, 1987a) provides an extremely rich set of data on ideas about the person in a patrilineal West African society. His account of concepts of the person among the Tallensi is firmly placed in the Maussian tradition. Fortes's essay on "The Concept of the Person" (1987a) begins with a reference to Mauss's 1938 lecture, and a description of going, together with Edward Evans-Pritchard, to meet Mauss at his hotel in London on that occasion. Fortes's own essay was, appropriately enough, delivered back to French anthropology in the form of a seminar to the Centre National de la Recherche Scientifique (CNRS) in Paris in 1971. Several times, Fortes alludes to Mauss's emphasis on the social derivation of concepts of the person (e.g. 1987a: 249, 252–3). He concludes that, for the Tallensi,

Personhood comes thus to be in its essence externally oriented. Self awareness means, in the first place, awareness of the self as a *personne morale* rather than as an idiosyncratic individual (1987a: 285; original italics).

This is predicated on a Maussian analysis.

Fortes describes how, for the Tallensi, birth is only the beginning of the process of becoming a complete person, providing, as he puts it, "the minimum quantum of personhood" (1987a: 261). Children are not necessarily named or placed under the care of their ancestral guardian until a younger sibling is born (1987a: 261). It is really only after a child is weaned and has a younger sibling that he or she is regarded as a potential person.

If birth is just the starting point of the attainment of full personhood, Fortes emphasizes that it is only after somebody has died that the true nature of his or her personhood can be ascertained. Through divination, death reveals whether full personhood has been achieved – if the ancestors have caused death, the deceased deserves a proper funeral and will in turn attain ancestorhood (1987a: 257, 265). Between birth and the attainment of ancestor status, the achievement of full personhood is a very gradual process. It must begin with birth "to a properly married mother in his father's house, as a legitimate member of the father's patrilineage and clan" (1987a: 271). The person must live long enough to marry and have children, and achieve the appropriate social relations and offices through the benevolence of his own ancestral guardian. Significantly, Fortes notes that, for the Tallensi, only men can attain full personhood, and that this is a life's work, demonstrated in the assumption of the status of male household head with full ritual and jural authority over all his dependents (that is, women and children), and in independent ownership of resources (1987a: 271).

There is a clear sense in which Tallensi notions of personhood put an extreme emphasis on continuity between members of one patrilineage. The place of the person in Tallensi society is determined at birth by his or her genealogical position in the descent group; members of the descent group embody lineage continuity – indeed, from birth they are ideally on their way to becoming ancestors; and lineage members are structurally alike.

The Tallensi recognize, of course, that individual life histories will differ from each other. This is partly expressed in the notion of *Yin*, good destiny, which differs for each person and is governed by the unique configuration of ancestors who guard that person's life course (1983: 21). This good destiny explains the particular coincidences and accidents of a person's life (1983: 19). Fortes emphasizes that this destiny is very much an expression of lineage continuity. If a man behaves with appropriate filial piety and makes the correct offerings to the ancestors, he will in return be blessed with good fortune, with sons and grandsons, and eventually achieve ancestorhood himself. A good destiny is, therefore, an indication of proper moral relations with parents and with the ancestors (1983: 25). But not everyone has an independent *Yin*. A man's *Yin* emerges only after marriage when he achieves adult status, and it grows as he becomes involved in full social relations. Before this, a man's *Yin* is governed by that of his father. Women never have their own independent *Yin,* and this reflects the fact that they never achieve full religious or jural autonomy – they begin life under the authority of their father, and after marriage this authority transfers to their husband (1983: 19).

If *Yin* reflects the benevolent powers of the ancestors, and is the expression of the person's continuity with other members of the descent group, there is another kind of destiny that has a more malevolent influence. This is the *Nuor-Yin,* or evil prenatal destiny, which, in the case of children, is actually that of their mother. Fortes describes how the victims of this force are typically "out on a limb" (1983: 17) – they are the young, the defective, and women – in other words, those who are less than fully incorporated into a lineage. And, in contrast to good destiny, this force indicates a failure in relations between kin, between lineage members, and between ancestors and descendants (1983: 34). It is symptomatic of this disruption to lineage continuity that *Nuor-Yin* is typically attributed as the cause of death in young people and of infertility in women (1983: 15–18).

My account of Tallensi personhood leaves out a great deal of the original ethnography. But the point I want to draw out is that even though

Tallensi notions of the person and ancestor worship strongly express the idea that lineage members are basically alike and continuous with each other, the concept of *Nuor-Yin* to some extent disrupts this. For what connects lineage members to each other are their patrilineal ties; what divides them are ties to their mothers (what Fortes calls *complementary filiation*). These are individuating ties. Fortes emphasizes that evil prenatal destiny afflicts those who are most dissociated from kin and lineage – the young and women. In this patrilineal society, women are always to some extent located between the lineage of their father and that of their husband (it is significant that both sets of kin carry out funerary rituals for women; see Fortes 1987a: 275).[1] In the sense that a woman's place in a lineage is partly defined by her husband and partly by her father, and not fully by either, we might say that her identity is less merged with the descent group and more individuated than that of men. This individuality is marked in the further sense that women are the potential victims of the capriciousness of their own evil prenatal destiny, which, in causing infertility, can further dissociate them from the lineage of their husbands.

But there is no reason to suggest that women are necessarily more likely to be attributed with individualizing traits than men in a patrilineal society. If we turn to another strongly patrilineal case, that of villagers in Hong Kong in the late 1970s, as described by Rubie Watson (1986), we find that exactly the reverse is true. Here, once again, it seems that women cannot attain full personhood, but this does not mean that they are inherently more individualized than men. Watson analyzes naming practices among these rural villagers. Here women are thought of as outsiders

---

[1] Fortes's formulation is somewhat different from mine. He makes clear that women remain jural and ritual minors throughout life, and never attain full personhood (1987a: 264). He also emphasizes that women's membership of their own patrilineage never lapses (1987a: 263), and suggests that they have a "dual social personality as wife on the one hand and daughter on the other." (1987a: 274).

and marginal to the exogamous patrilineage; after marriage, a couple live in the husband's natal home (1986: 620). Watson shows how, as they move through life, men gradually acquire more and more names as they acquire new roles and responsibilities. These names mark the social transitions of men's life course. Infant boys receive a personal name at the age of one month, as do girls. But whereas girls' names tend to be negative and stereotypical rather than individuating, for example "little mistake" or "to endure," boys' names are distinctive, individuating, and flattering; they convey learning and status. Men choose another name for themselves when they marry (1986: 621). They also acquire a nickname that is highly personalized, and they may bestow nicknames on others, and in doing so display their cleverness and wit. As they get older, men are also given courtesy names that mark their social and economic status, and eventually, after they die, they acquire a posthumous name (1986: 623–6).

Far from acquiring names as they get older, women tend to lose their individual identity. They are called by a kin term, addressed as "mother of . . . " or "grandmother of . . . " (a teknonym) or a category term, and they lose their own personal name on marriage. Thus terms of address for adult women are dependent on the position of their husband in the lineage. Women are not named and they do not name others. In old age, women do not, like men, gain individuality, but lose it. They are often addressed or referred to simply as "old woman." And unlike men, they have no name on their tombstone, and no separate ancestral tablet (1986: 626–8).

Watson draws a contrast between women as outsiders who are marginal to the identity of the lineage, and whose personhood and identity are largely ascribed, and men, whose personhood grows and accumulates through life, and for whom personhood is both ascribed and achieved. In this account, a woman has no public identity apart from her husband's; she cannot attain full personhood in local terms. This contrast is summarized in the fact that whereas men have the power to name themselves and others, women do not – they cannot become unique individuals (1986: 626–8).

The Hong Kong example demonstrates that although gender, personhood, and kinship are apparently mutually constituted, there is no obvious or simple correlation between them. For the Tallensi, full personhood is very much a matter of achieving one's appropriate position in a lineage. Individuality is conceived as a force that upsets lineage continuity. In Watson's depiction of her particular case study, it appears that full personhood involves the expression of individual qualities *in addition* to one's lineage position, and that women are thought to lack the capacity for this. Here individuality enhances the continuity of the lineage rather than detracting from it. Although kinship in both cases might be described in terms of patrilineality and virilocality, individuality is ascribed to women in one case and men in the other.

The Partible Person

The strong contrastive theme between the kinds of personhood found in the West and those in non-Western societies – a theme that underlies the analyses of Mauss, Dumont, and Fortes – has continued to shape more recent studies. Perhaps the most influential of these is Strathern's *The Gender of the Gift* (1988). In Chapter 5, I again take up the Melanesian notions of the person described by Strathern, in the context of an analysis of kinship that foregrounds ideas about bodily substance. Here I want briefly to delineate some of the features of personhood in Melanesia described by Strathern, and to dwell on the contrast she proposes with Western notions.

In a much quoted passage, Strathern draws a sharp distinction between the person in Melanesia and Western individualism:

Far from being regarded as unique entities, Melanesian persons are as dividually as they are individually conceived. They contain a generalized sociality within. Indeed, persons are frequently constructed as the plural and composite site of the relationships that produced them. The singular person can be imagined as social microcosm (Strathern 1988: 13).

In the Melanesian cases analyzed by Strathern, persons are inherently social. They are not the repository of a unitary or bounded identity but rather are composed of social relations, and in this sense can be thought of as "dividual" or "partible" entitites. Indeed, much of the effort of puberty and intitiation rituals is to draw out of persons the social relations within them, which are imprinted on the body. But here there is a crucial distinction from the conventional anthropological figure of the person as:

. . . a locus of roles, a constellation of statuses. In the Melanesian image, a series of events is being revealed in the body, which becomes thereby composed of the specific historical actions of social others: what people have or have not done to or for one (Strathern 1988: 132).

Social interactions are registered in each person, but these interactions are subject to change and to further intervention, and this in turn determines how relations are conducted (cf. Strathern 1988: 131–2).

Part of Strathern's aim is to explicate the contrast between the logic of social relations in Melanesia and in the West. This is encapsulated in the contrast between gift and commodity exchange – the one based on relations between people or subjects, the other on relations between objects. While the underlying premise of a gift economy is the expansion of social relations, the logic of a commodity economy depends on the appropriation of goods (1988: 143). This is expressed in terms of a different kind of relation between persons and things:

[I]f in a commodity economy things and persons assume the social form of things, then in a gift economy they assume the social form of persons (Strathern 1988: 134, italics removed; adapted from Gregory 1982: 41).

The commodity logic extends to Western notions of the person. Here persons own themselves and their own products. As Strathern notes, the Marxist critique of capitalism rests on the idea that persons have a natural right to the products of their own labor: "they are the authors of their acts" (1988: 142). They are also the owners of their own bodies, and of their bodies' parts. The Western person may be modified through external relations, but is defined by the internal attributes on which the uniqueness of each individual is premised (Strathern 1988: 57, 135). In this sense, Strathern suggests, the Western person is a homologue of society. In the same way as society is thought to domesticate nature and harness nature's resources, the internal attributes of persons constitute their "natural resources," and like the "natural" resources of nature, are conceived as "things." Thus persons are thought of "as original proprietors of themselves" (1988: 135).

Inevitably, I have omitted much from this account of Strathern's comparative endeavor. Crucial to her exposition is a sensitivity to what she calls the "controlled fiction" of analysis – the artificiality by which the apparent simplicity of the world being depicted by anthropologists is rendered in what appear to be *theoretically* complex ways. Strathern seeks "another mode by which to reveal the complexities of social life" (1988: 7), one that sets up "an internal dialogue" within the analysis itself (1988: 7). This is achieved through the deployment of a number of paired analytic oppositions that run through her exposition. The gift/commodity contrast is one axis that she uses in this way. The others are the classic we/they opposition of anthropology, and the contrasting perspectives of anthropologist and feminist. As she makes clear, these oppositions are rooted in Western analytic discourses. Part of Strathern's aim is precisely to expose what is taken for granted in anthropology's academic theorizing: "I choose to show the contextualized nature of indigenous constructs by exposing the contextualized nature of analytical ones" (1988: 8). It is to this end that she juxtaposes anthropological discourses with feminist ones (1988: 4–11).

With this in mind, it may be worth looking more closely at Western notions of the person. The persuasiveness of Strathern's image of the partible person partly rests on the stong contrast between Westerners, for whom relations are somehow added to the person, and Melanesians, for whom relations are intrinsic, or prior, to personhood, and for whom social effort is expended precisely on drawing such intrinsic relations out of the person. This invites the conclusion that whereas Westerners emphasize unique, bounded individuals, Melanesians accentuate relations. Although, here, once again, it is worth drawing attention to the sources from which this image of the person in the West is drawn – especially to the prominence of legal and philosophical discourses about property and ownership.[2]

On Not Being a Crocodile, and Posthumous Conception

Whereas in many cultures birth is viewed as a process, in which characteristics and attributes are gradually acquired (see Bloch 1993; Carsten 1995a), the Western view apparently emphasizes the unique potentiality of each human being, and how this potentiality is already present from the moment of birth, and some would argue, from the very moment of conception. Maurice Bloch (1988, 1993) has suggested that the extreme emphasis expressed in Western medical and legal contexts on the precise moment at which a person is born or dies is one expression of the bounded individuality of the person. These concerns are particularly evident in medical and ethical debates surrounding death and birth. The importance of the particular moment at which a person comes into being is often the focus of emotionally charged discussion in the context of abortion and embryo research (see Franklin 1993).

---

[2] The analytic siginificance of Western notions of property, ownership, and intellectual property rights are the focus of much of Strathern's more recent work (see Strathern 1996, 1999a).

The anthropological assumptions about the individuality of personhood in the West are certainly borne out by the religous and ethical concerns over a person's "right" to die and his or her "right" to be born. If abortion is one familiar context in which these concerns are expressed, at the other end of the human life span, euthanasia seems to generate just as much moral fervor. What is at issue here is precisely the right of one individual to intercede for another and to curtail that other's life. However degraded their quality of life or "unpersonlike" an individual has become, there is a supreme value placed on individual life itself.

Following Bloch (1988), I suggest that it may be potentially misleading to overstate the contrast between Western and non-Western personhood. Alexandra Ouroussoff (1993) convincingly argues that anthropological assumptions about Western individualism derive from a tradition of philosophic liberalism, of which anthropology is itself part, rather than from an ethnography of Western people's lived experience in specific contexts. Using her own research on behavior in a multinational manufacturing company, she demonstrates how markedly people's actual experience diverges from this abstracted theory. While fully acknowledging the importance of the value of individualism in the West, and its prominent expression in many legal, medical, philosophical, and religious discourses, it is important to recognize that Western notions of the person express other values too. These are present in very familiar and everyday contexts, and they also evoke qualities similar to those that anthropologists have been accustomed to attribute to persons in non-Western cultures. In a game with her father, my then-four-year-old daughter grew tired of him playing the role of a crocodile: "No, no, stop being a crocodile, daddy," she admonished him, "be a person, be yourself, be a daddy." This succinctly phrased and utterly mundane demand makes clear how, for this small child (and, no doubt, most others), personhood, being "oneself," and being a father – in other words, being a relation – are quite intertwined.

If we return to the medical contexts to which I briefly alluded above, I think it is possible to perceive something more being expressed than simply the value of each unique and bounded individual identity. The case of Diane Blood, to which I have already referred, and which received prominent coverage in the British press between 1996 and 1997, highlights some interesting issues in terms of debated attributes of the person (cf. Simpson 2001). The case concerned Diane Blood's disputed right to conceive a child by artificial insemination using the sperm of her dead husband. Stephen Blood died a few days after contracting bacterial meningitis in 1995. His sperm had been removed while he was in a coma and on life-support machines. Although the couple had been trying to conceive a child for two months prior to his illness, no formal written consent for the removal of the sperm or for artificial insemination had been obtained. It was on these grounds, and because Stephen Blood had not had the opportunity to be counseled as required under British law, that the Human Fertilisation and Embryology Authority (HFEA) refused to grant permission for Diane Blood to undergo artificial insemination using her husband's sperm.[3] This decision was challenged in the High Court but dismissed on the same grounds in October 1996.

While the legal judgments focused on the individual rights of Stephen Blood to his own sperm, Diane Blood expressed her intention to take the case to the Court of Appeal in terms of her own rights: "I think that I have the most right of anybody to my husband's sperm and I desperately wanted his baby" (*The Guardian* 18.10.96). Her fight commanded not only the support of Stephen Blood's parents, but also that of several leading fertility experts and commentators, and of Baroness Warnock, who had chaired the committee that led to the establishment of the HFEA. Baroness Warnock was reported to blame herself because "we didn't think of the kind of contingency which has actually arisen" (*The Guardian* 18.10.96). Sir Stephen Brown, president of the High Court's Family Division, was

---

[3] The HFEA is a British government body established under the terms of the Human Fertilisation and Embryology Act (1990). The Agency has jurisdiction over fertility treatment, control of donated eggs and sperm, and research on human embryos.

clearly sympathetic: "My heart goes out to this applicant who wishes to preserve an essential part of her late beloved husband. The refusal to permit her to do so is for her in the nature of a double bereavement. It stirs the emotions and evokes what I believe to be universal sympathy for the applicant." In the same newspaper report, "Leading fertility expert" Lord Winston described the decision of the High Court as "cruel and unnatural" (*The Guardian* 18.10.96).

In the face of widespread public support for Diane Blood's cause, there were, however, some dissenters. In a comment piece in *The Guardian*, Martin Kettle made a significant analogy between Stephen Blood's sperm and property:

The dead cannot clarify their intentions. That is why in the parallel context of property, wills are so important and probate law so meticulous. Mr Blood's sperm is no different. He did not leave the written consent the law requires, so his intentions are not proved (*The Guardian* 23.11.96).

In contrast to Lord Winston, Kettle argued that it was neither right nor natural for Diane Blood to conceive her child "with a dead father." In fact, it was "decidedly creepy" and "morbid." Questioning Diane Blood's "inalienable right to conceive," Kettle drew attention instead to the importance of gaining informed consent for the removal of the sperm, and to the child's right to a living father. Here the "rights" of specific individuals were held to conflict with each other.

In November 1996, the HFEA ruled that Diane Blood could not legally export her husband's sperm to Belgium for use there. Once again, the Authority cited the lack of written consent as the grounds for this decision:

There is a clear requirement for the written and effective consent of a man after he has had the opportunity to receive counselling and after he has had a proper opportunity to consider the implications of a posthumous birth (HFEA statement cited in *The Guardian* 23.11.96).

This decision was reportedly influenced by a letter from Stuart Horner, chair of the British Medical Association's ethics committee, which expressed concern about a possible erosion of "the doctrine of informed consent, which is central to medical ethics." Significantly, the concern drew a parallel with organ donation, and raised the possibility of organs being removed from unconscious patients. Reportedly, there was a stark contrast here between the views of the clinicians seeking to help "sometimes desperate individuals to fulfil themselves through having children" and "the inhuman general ethical principles that get in the way" (*The Guardian* 23.11.96).

In February 1997, an Appeal Court judgment upheld Diane Blood's right as a European Community citizen to have medical treatment in another member state. She was granted permission to export her husband's sperm to Belgium and to have treatment there. At the same time, however, the Appeal Court forestalled the possibility of further similar applications by ruling that the extraction and storage of the sperm without Stephen Blood's consent had been unlawful. The bar to further cases suggests that the decision to allow Diane Blood to seek treatment abroad was at least in part a response to the public support she had received. Professor Ian Craft, director of the London Gynaecology and Infertility Centre, called the decision a "fudge," blaming poorly drafted and inflexible legislation, as well as a "restrictive" and "intransigent" HFEA. Pointing out that women have the right to undergo termination of a pregnancy or a hysterectomy without their partner's permission, he argued that preventing a woman from becoming pregnant in such circumstances was an infringement of individual freedom (*The Guardian* 7.2.97).

The legal judgments and debates in this case clearly hinged on the rights of the individual to his or her own body and its parts. They expressed rather literally a notion of persons as "the authors of their acts" (Strathern 1988: 142) or as "proprietors of themselves" (1988: 135). But in the intense public debate that the case generated, other themes came to the fore. Underlying much of the popular concern was sympathy for

Diane Blood's own desire to conceive a child by her dead husband, and thereby to perpetuate his relational identity as a husband and a potential father (see also Simpson 2001: 3). Indeed, this is precisely what is referred to in Sir Stephen Brown's statement at the time of the High Court ruling. And it is a concern for this relational identity that is at the center of Diane Blood's subsequent efforts, once her son had been born, to effect a change in British law so that Stephen Blood's name might appear as father on her son's birth certificate.[4] The ethical concerns over this case certainly did focus on the individual's rights to ownership of his own body and the bounded individuality of Diane Blood's deceased husband. Nevertheless, the considerable public sympathy generated by Diane Blood's predicament and the distaste voiced for an excessively legalistic interpretation of events suggest that, in certain contexts at least, death may not be simply a punctual moment, and that a more popularly understood relational identity may conflict with a legally defined individuality.

Joined-Up Western Persons

The ethical issues raised by Diane Blood's application to use her deceased husband's sperm were compared by at least one commentator to those surrounding organ donation. The parallel is worth pursuing further. Ray Abrahams (1990) discusses the concerns of those involved in kidney transplants. At issue here is precisely the boundedness of the personhood of the donor and of the recipient.[5] In cases of live donation between kin,

---

[4] For children conceived after their fathers' death before 2003, the father's name was left unrecorded (*Guardian*, 24.04.01; *Independent* 1.03.03). The significance of this absence for Diane Blood bears out Bob Simpson's observation that "The posthumously conceived child is both the realization of the father's intent and a repository for the memory of him" (2001: 3).

[5] I am grateful to Joni Wilson for bringing the issue of organ donation, as well as Abrahams' article, to my attention. Wilson's unpublished Ph.D thesis (Wilson 2000) constitutes a more extensive anthropological exploration of the issues raised by organ donation than I can summarize here.

doctors and legislators have expressed concern about a perceived intensi-
fication of the already existing tie between donor and recipient. This in-
tensification is especially apparent when donor and recipient are siblings
(1990: 137). The reported worry about "incestuous" links created in this
way is replicated in a different form when the transplanted organ comes
from the body of a dead donor. Here what is at issue is not the intensi-
fication of already existing ties beyond what is perceived as appropriate,
but the creation of new links through donation. Abrahams reports that
relatives of the deceased donor may "wish to establish links with the recipient in whom they see the donor as, in some sense, living on" (1990: 132).
The medical professionals involved, however, seek to control the flow of
information between the donor's family and recipient in order to protect
the latter from possible demands and to prevent relations from developing. In particular, they discourage any idea of continuity between the
deceased donor and the recipient (Abrahams 1990: 142–3; Wilson 2000).

In spite of the expressed concerns of the medical professionals, and
their attempts to limit the possible contact between donor families and
recipients, it is apparent from an American study cited by Abrahams that
bereaved relatives do perceive the donor as, in some sense, living on in
the recipient (Abrahams 1990: 143; Fulton, Fulton, and Simmons 1977).
This sense of immortality or continuity is expressed in both physical and
spiritual terms. Nor are these expressions of the unboundedness of the
person confined to donors. Abrahams discusses the concerns articulated
by a British heart transplant patient over the possibility that, in acquiring another person's heart, she might become somebody different, who
would feel differently about her fiancé.

This material is suggestive for several reasons. Once again, we are
confronted with a context in which a person's "punctual" death may
be qualified by the relatives' sense of that person's continuity in the body
of another. Although the context seems rather exotic, the idea is all too
familiar. A similar continuity between bodies and persons is expressed
each time adults remark upon a child's resemblance to aspects of a dead

relative's appearance or behavior. But perhaps there is something more to the fact that these connections are apparently evoked in an idiom of kinship. In the case of a boy whose heart was given to a girl in a transplant operation, when the two fathers met, the father of the boy told the father of the girl how they had always wanted a girl, "so now we're going to have her and share her with you" (Fox and Swazey 1978: 32; cited in Abrahams 1990: 140).

Abrahams focuses on doctors' desire to control and limit the formation of such ties, which he relates to:

... the nature of our kinship system, in which, for economic and other reasons, people generally appear keen to limit their kinship ties rather than extend them (Abrahams 1990: 141).

The desire to limit kinship ties seems, however, less than self-evident – in the cases cited, it also appears to be distinctly one-sided. My final example is one in which, in the face of considerable emotional pain and personal risk, the extension of kinship ties is deliberately sought out.

In late 1998, in Scotland, I interviewed a woman in her fifties who had been adopted as a baby.[6] About ten years before this, as the mother of several grown children, she had begun a search for her birth kin. This woman described to me the process of searching for and eventually making contact with her birth kin. One of the many poignant aspects of this story was that although her birth father's name was on her birth certificate (an unusual circumstance in cases of illegitimate births of that era), when she eventually found him, he repeatedly denied to her that he

---

[6] I conducted thirteen interviews in 1997–8 with adults who had experience of reunion between adoptees and birth kin in the recent past. Most of these interviews were with adult women adoptees in their midtwenties to early sixties. Initial contacts were made with the help of a Scottish nongovernment organization which in the past had functioned as an adoption agency, and more recently exercised a number of "social work" functions, including helping people to trace birth kin from whom they had been separated. Names and some details of personal biographies have been changed in order to protect the privacy of those concerned (see Carsten 2000b).

was her father. Eventually, in an effort to "stop the lies," as she put it, she underwent DNA screening together with a half brother on her father's side. The results were apparently conclusive – her birth father's identity was confirmed. But in another poignant twist, by the time the results came through, her father had died. I was struck by the apparent futility of the procedure. As she told me, she had wanted the results to "waft them under his nose"; by the time she got them, "he didn't have a nose to waft them under." But long before undergoing testing, she had known that he was, as she put it, "a chancer," "someone who would sell something worth 50p for 50 pounds." What then was she to gain by confirming his identity as her birth father?

This is one of a number of cases I could cite in which adults who were adopted in childhood have with considerable trouble, and often quite traumatic results, sought out their birth kin. What is very striking about these cases is that, although the contacts with birth kin often prove extremely difficult and painful, and the adoptees make no attempt to hide or deny this, they never voice regret at having initiated the process. In answer to perhaps the simplest and most obvious question, why did they feel the need to go through such a search, respondents simply say, "in order to know who I am," "to find out where I came from," or "to be complete." It is important to emphasize that in many cases the adoptees gave these responses with the full knowledge that the relationships they had sought would never be particularly successful or easy. The adoptees did not perceive these relationships to be in any sense equivalent to those that many of them had with their adopted kin or with their own birth children. Most of those whom I interviewed no longer held (and many had never held) any illusions about the potential of the relations they had established with their birth kin.

The paramount importance of discovering "who one is" or "where one came from" expresses the sense of incompleteness experienced by at least some adoptees who grew up with no knowledge of their birth kin. This incompleteness or deficit should make us pause. Another very striking aspect of the lives of those whom I interviewed was the fact that most of them were deeply embedded in kin relations. Not only were the majority either married or in stable partnerships that obviously gave them support and satisfaction, most also had children of their own. And they also maintained relations with their adopted kin, who in many but not all cases were spoken of with considerable warmth. Going to interview people in their own homes, I was often struck by the large number of family photographs on prominent display. These were hardly people who were "out on a limb," to recall Fortes's phrase.

I am not suggesting here that the boundedness of the individual or individual rights of ownership are not prominent themes of Western discourse. To do so would clearly be quite misleading. It is obviously striking that Diane Blood's legal struggle to acquire control of her husband's sperm, like the problematic issues at stake when a heart donor is perceived to live on in a recipient, is at least in some contexts articulated in terms of a discourse on property and individual rights.[7] Bob Simpson has pointed out the considerable irony of the fact that although Diane Blood's case apparently foregrounds strongly normative aspects of kinship, legally it was won "on the grounds that the free movement of 'goods and services' within the European Union was being denied" (Simpson 2001: 13).

In the case of adoption, it was precisely the obvious contrast between Western adoption, which signals the full relinquishing of parental rights on the part of birth parents, and Malay fostering, which is both very frequent and does not involve the assumption of exclusive parental rights, that motivated me to undertake research on adoption reunions in Scotland. Whereas in the West "missing" birth parents often appear to occupy a very prominent place in the imaginary world of child and adult adoptees, it is hard to imagine a Malay adult who has been fostered in childhood seeking out her birth parents in the way I have described here.

---

[7] I am grateful to Michael Lambek for focusing my attention on this point.

This is most obviously unlikely because the connections to birth parents would have been maintained alongside those to foster parents. "Finding" one's birth parents would thus take on quite different meanings, and knowledge of kin connections or origins would not have the revelatory force that it appears to have in the Scottish contexts that I investigated. One might say that in the Malay case, such knowledge does not have the same power to constitute or dislodge a person's sense of her own identity.

Here I draw on Strathern's (1999b) argument that, in Euro-American contexts, acquiring certain kinds of knowledge about one's ancestry implies acquiring identity. Strathern also argues that this kind of knowledge has an immediate effect – once obtained, it cannot be rejected or put aside: "knowledge creates relationships: the relationship comes into being when the knowledge does" (1999b: 78). This is the case, she suggests, whether one admits the relation or not. The immediacy of these effects are quite apparent in the accounts of reunions that I collected. But one might add that these effects are already prefigured by the decision to search for birth kin and the process of undergoing such a search. The decision *not* to seek out birth kin could of course be seen as equally constitutive of identity. If knowing one's parentage is "constitutive information" (1999b: 69), then knowledge that one is adopted (whether or not one pursues birth ties) has the power to create, and also potentially to dislodge, a sense of self.

I pursue the relation between knowledge and kinship further in Chapter 7. But is it possible to take account of the sense of incompleteness, of the need expressed by some adoptees to discover their own identity through learning about and meeting birth kin, and of the apparent sense of satisfaction this brought? This involves paying close attention to the ways in which this sense is articulated in the idiom of kinship. Perhaps the most obvious conclusion to draw from these stories of adoptees' searches for their birth kin, which I take up again in Chapter 6, is the extent to which kinship is intrinsic to personhood. Without knowledge of a birth mother, and to a lesser extent knowledge of a birth father, these people's sense of self is apparently fractured and partial. And this suggests a notion of personhood where kinship is not simply added to bounded individuality, but one where kin relations are perceived as intrinsic to the self. It is precisely the sense that something was missing in their own personhood that is strongly articulated by those who have undergone searches for their birth kin.

Conclusions

I have delineated several contexts in which the boundedness and the strong individuality of the Western person are called into question. The Western "relational person" who comes to the fore when adoptees seek reunions with birth kin, in cases of organ donation or when a widow attempts to have a child by her deceased husband, may be regarded perhaps as responses to unusual circumstances. But I would argue to the contrary. It is the very ordinary quality of this relationality that has obscured it from view. And it was precisely this everyday sense of relationality that was mobilized in the widespread sympathetic public response to Diane Blood's predicament in contrast to what was perceived as an excessively legalistic adherence to the issue of consent.[8]

Because anthropologists have looked to philosophy, jurisprudence, and theology in their consideration of personhood in the West, they have emphasized the notion of an abstract and legally defined entity, the bounded individual with rights over property and person, as the dominant Western construct. In doing so, they have obscured the most obvious contexts in which relationality as an aspect of personhood is expressed. Not surprisingly, these contexts involve a consideration of kinship; the relations that are perceived as being intrinsic to the person, but also as capable of overcoming the boundedness of particular bodies and persons, are evoked in

---

[8]   Simpson (2001: 11–12) rightly underlines how Diane Blood's status as young widow was one source of this public sympathy and made her desire to commemorate her husband by having his child apparently self-evident.

an idiom of kinship in its broadest sense. And these contexts are precisely the ones upon which anthropologists have focused in their studies of personhood in non-Western cultures.

I suggest that just as personhood became in the 1980s a means to reformulate and critique kinship, we can now use this reformulated version of kinship to upset our assumptions about personhood. In suggesting that we might qualify the strong contrast between Western individualism and non-Western dividualism, I am not implying that such contrasts cannot serve analytic ends. As Strathern makes clear, however fictional, they clearly do. The destabilization of a Western/non-Western opposition is of course merely the mirror image of an analytic strategy founded on the contrastive mode, and is thus equally dependent on it. In the following chapter, I pursue a similar comparative strategy by tracing the geographic wanderings and analytic deployment of another concept that has been closely linked to that of personhood and, like personhood, has been central to recent reformulations of kinship: bodily substance.

FIVE

Uses and Abuses of Substance

In the shift from kinship to relatedness, we have seen how a focus on the person, gender, and house provided ways to open up kinship to new kinds of analysis. One other key term, used by anthropologists to dismantle kinship in its more classic guises, has been *substance*. In this enterprise, David Schneider's work was highly influential. *Substance* was one of Schneider's key terms, which he used to unlock the cultural meanings of *American Kinship* (1980). Anthropologists working in India and Papua New Guinea, among other places, have adopted substance as a way of understanding kinship in more processual terms, looking at how persons were constituted through their relations with others.

Substance was a kind of catch-all term that can be used to trace the bodily transformation of food into blood, sexual fluids, sweat, and saliva, and to analyze how these passed from person to person through eating together, living in houses, having sexual relations, and performing ritual exchanges. It thus necessarily links together some of the topics I have covered in previous chapters – the house and feeding, personhood and relations, bodies, and gender. In this chapter, I explore exactly how and why anthropologists have used the term *substance*, and where this focus has taken the study of kinship. I begin with some brief examples before putting substance into its anthropological context.

We saw in the previous chapter how anthropological comparisons of the person turned on a quite stark opposition between dividual non-Western persons and Western individuals. A similar dichotomy runs through anthropological analyses of bodily substance. In the West, substance was seen as immutable and permanent, whereas in non-Western cases substance was depicted as inherently fluid and transformable. Thus, for example, E. Valentine Daniel has described in his monograph, *Fluid Signs* (1984), how Tamils of South India do not think of blood, milk, and sexual fluids as separate entities but permutations of each other. These bodily substances are essentially fluid and transformable as they combine, mix, separate, and recombine, both within particular bodies and through the processes of contact between persons that occur in daily life. Coresidence, food, eating, and sex are crucial vectors of these bodily transformations, and of the moral and spiritual qualities that accompany them. And there are elaborate rules and distinctions governing both the substances themselves and the activities through which they may be transferred.

To take another example, in her highly influential comparative study *The Gender of the Gift* (1988), Marilyn Strathern analyzes how in different Melanesian cultures, particular substances, such as food, blood, milk, and semen, are not merely transformable into each other, they take different male and female forms. These are detachable from particular bodies; they circulate and are exchanged, and they can be both a source of replenishment for the other sex and also a potential danger. Such bodily substances, and other objects and substances that, by analogy, are associated with them, are invested with particular symbolic significance that is central to distinctions of gender.

The contrast that anthropologists have depicted between an image of bodily substance as fluid and mutable, and one in which is it permanent and fixed is, as I shall show, linked to the contrast anthropologists have made between ideas of the person in the West and in the non-West. Anthropological discussions about bodies and about persons have often complemented each other and been part of a single larger description. Personhood and substance have in fact been closely linked in anthropological analyses and in the analytic work that they enabled.

It is of course significant that anthropologists can make a single term cover such an apparently disparate set of entities and bodily processes as I have already sketched. *The Oxford English Dictionary* lists twenty-three separate meanings for *substance*, covering three full pages. Several of these meanings clearly overlap or relate very closely to each other. Nevertheless, there are some important distinctions between *substance* as "essential nature" or "essence"; as a "separate distinct thing"; as "that which underlies phenomena"; as "matter or subject matter"; as "material of which a physical thing consists"; as "matter or tissue composing an animal body part or organ"; as "any corporeal matter"; as a "solid or real thing (opposed to appearance or shadow)"; as a "vital part"; as "what gives a thing its character"; and as "the consistency of a fluid." I have selected just some of the *OED*'s long list of meanings. These are some of the meanings that seem to have relevance for an examination of the uses to which *substance* has been put in the anthropological study of kinship. We can reduce the *OED*'s list of meanings to four broader categories: vital part or essence; separate distinct thing; that which underlies phenomena; and corporeal matter. All of these distinct meanings have some bearing on anthropological understandings. Indeed, the utility of *substance* as a term is due largely to the very breadth of meanings that I have delineated.

Before looking in detail at the meanings ascribed to *substance* and the cultural contexts to which they have been applied, I want to sketch out some of the term's anthropological history.

Substance in American Kinship

Schneider was perhaps the first anthropologist to use *substance* as an analytic term in relation to kinship. In *American Kinship: A Cultural Account* (1980), Schneider argued that "relatives" were defined by "blood," and that "[t]he blood relationship, as it is defined in American kinship, is formulated in concrete, biogenetic terms" (Schneider 1980: 23). Each parent contributes one half of the biogenetic substance of his or her child. "The blood relationship is thus a relationship of substance, of shared biogenetic material" (1980: 25). Schneider noted two crucial properties of such relationships. First, blood endures, and cannot be terminated; blood relationships cannot be lost or severed. Even if parents disown their children, or siblings cease to communicate, the biological relationship remains unaltered. Blood relatives remain blood relatives. Second, "kinship is whatever the biogenetic relationship is. If science discovers new facts about biogenetic relationship, then that is what kinship is, and was all along, although it may not have been known at the time" (1980: 23).

The first point to emphasize about Schneider's analytic strategy is the way he moves between "blood" and "biogenetic substance" – also rendered as "natural substance." Thus he writes, "[t]wo blood relatives are 'related' by the fact that they share in some degree the stuff of a particular heredity. Each has a portion of the natural, genetic substance" (1980: 24). Blood is the symbol for biogenetic substance, which he also calls "the stuff of a particular heredity" and "the natural genetic substance" (1980: 24). But what is remarkable in this rendering of American kinship is that blood and biogenetic substance are quite unexplored as symbols; one could, after all, easily imagine a whole book to be written on American notions of blood.

Schneider's shift from blood to biogenetic substance (in other words, the relationship between the symbol and what is allegedly symbolized) is also unexamined. It is, for example, not at all clear that biogenetic heredity, or substance, is not itself a symbol in American culture. It may be that recent scientific and popular discourses in which the biogenetic components of heredity have been particularly prominent have made Schneider's shift from blood to heredity, and from heredity to genetic substance, appear less than self-evident. If that is the case, this only underlines the point that there is something worth examining here.

Jeanette Edwards's (1993) observations from northwest England about what is transferred from mother to child through the placenta are suggestive in this context. Her informants speculate on the effect on a baby of being nurtured in an artificial womb in the laboratory. Such a baby would not be connected to its mother or to her feelings.

Somebody somewhere must be creating this artificial womb. A baby reacts to what you're feeling – if your heartbeat is faster then the baby's heartbeat is faster. It could be fed on just vegetables – how would it react then, through the placenta – not what you fancy like crisps, or salad, or chewitts on the bus, like cravings at different times – vegetables, sweets, alcohol whatever it takes to make a baby. It will have no feelings because no feelings are going through it (Edwards 1993: 59).

The image of a baby born without feelings because it was never connected to maternal emotion and never received the effects of maternal cravings in the form of a packet of crisps or a glass of beer suggests something rather different from scientific discourse on biogenetic heredity. It is beyond the scope of the present chapter to explore the meanings of blood and of biogenetic substance in American culture. As Charis Thompson (2001) demonstrates through her analysis of practices and discourses in infertility clinics, "biological" kinship can be configured in a remarkable number of ways, as can the connections that are made between "social" and "biological" kinship. Her conclusion, that there is no "unique template" for biological kinship, suggests that the relationship between blood and biogenetic substance is less straightforward than Schneider seemed to assume.

This brings me to my second point about Schneider's analysis. Schneider argued that American kinship was built out of two elements: relationship as natural substance, and relationship as code for conduct. These elements were themselves derived from the two major orders of American culture: the order of nature, and the order of law (Schneider 1980: 29). Certain relationships existed by virtue of nature alone – for example, the natural or illegitimate child. Others, like husband and wife, were relatives in law alone. The third class of relatives were those defined by blood. These included father, mother, brother, sister, son, daughter, as well as aunt, uncle, niece, nephew, grandparent, grandchild, cousin, and so on. These derived from both nature and law, substance and code. Schneider's analysis thus not only suggested the combinatory power of substance and code in the category of "blood" relations, but also posited clear, strong boundaries between substance and code, and the two cultural orders from which they were derived, nature and law. Each could be clearly defined, and legitimacy was derived either from one or the other, or from both together – but one could attribute aspects to either one domain or the other. As Schneider himself put it:

It is a fundamental premise of the American kinship system that blood is a substance and that this is quite distinct from the kind of relationship or code for conduct which persons who share that substance, blood, are supposed to have. It is precisely on this distinction between relationship as *substance* and relationship as *code for conduct* that the classification of relatives in nature, relatives in law and those who are related in both nature and in law, the blood relatives, rests.... [T]hese two elements, substance and code for conduct, are quite distinct. Each can occur alone or they can occur in combination (Schneider 1980: 91, original italics).

It is this seemingly unproblematic distinction between the order of nature and the order of law, and between natural substance and code for conduct, that I would question here.

I cited a case from northwest England that renders the distinction between substance and code – between a biological basis for heredity, and maternal cravings for crisps or chewitts on a bus – difficult to draw. My questioning comes with other recent ethnographic examples from Britain and America in mind. The first is from Gerd Baumann's (1995) description of the mixed ethnic setting of the London suburb of Southall. Baumann describes how in Southall young Sikhs, Hindus, and Muslims, as well as Afro-Caribbeans and whites, all emphasize "cousin" relations to a remarkable degree – often in the absence of specific genealogical ties. Young people make claims to cousinship for a variety of reasons, saying "cousins are friends who are kin and kin who are friends" (Baumann 1995: 734). It is precisely the coincidence of nature and choice in the discourse about cousins that Baumann underlines. Cousins are sufficiently related to owe solidarity to each other, but distant enough to require a voluntaristic input.

This almost conscious blurring of the boundaries between the natural and the social orders bears some similarities with Kath Weston's description of gay American kinship ideology (Weston 1991, 1995). Gay coming-out stories foreground the traumatic experience of disruption to bonds of kinship that are supposed to be about "diffuse enduring solidarity." Weston's informants emphasize the enduring qualities of friendship in the face of an experience of kinship that involves the severance of "biological" ties when parents or other close kin refuse to acknowledge those who have revealed their sexuality. Reversing the terms of the dominant discourse of kinship – in which kinship ties necessarily imply permanence – in this context, ties that last, that is, those of friendship, are taken as demonstrating "proper" kinship. Once again, we might say that this discourse suggests a more or less conscious attempt to muddle the distinction between two cultural orders. Weston explicitly challenges the traditional anthropological ascription of one set of ties as "fictive," while Strathern has underlined how the critique of gay kinship makes explicit "the fact that there always was a choice as to whether or not biology is made the foundation of relationships" (Strathern 1993: 196, cited in Hayden 1995: 45).

I would not claim that these examples rule out the possibility of analyzing kinship in Schneider's terms; indeed, both Baumann and Weston fruitfully discuss their material in terms of Schneider's analysis. But such cases do suggest that the categorical separation, or even opposition, of the two orders, and of substance and code, is worthy of further examination. That much remains to be said about substance and about the relationship between substance and code is all the more critical when we trace what happened to substance when it was transferred from American kinship to India. For the relationship between substance and code was very much at issue when anthropologists compared India to America, or to "the West."

In the following sections of this chapter, I trace the passage of substance, from Schneider's original application of it, to India, and from India to Melanesia. My analysis focuses on the uses to which substance has been put in the analysis of kinship, rather than on what it means within any one particular culture.

Substance in India

On the one hand, I have suggested that the promise of *substance* as an analytic term lay to a considerable extent in its flexibility, which can be attributed to its multiple meanings in English. On the other hand, the separation or opposition of substance and code, which Schneider proposed, imposed a startling rigidity on the analysis of kinship undertaken in these terms. This rigidity becomes very clear when we look at the way substance came to be understood in the context of Indian notions of kinship and personhood. What is perhaps even more significant is that both the flexible and the rigid aspects of *substance* as an analytic term remained quite implicit and unexplored.

The ethnosociological model of India proposed by McKim Marriott, Ronald Inden, Ralph Nicholas, and others in the 1970s explicitly followed the logic of Schneider's analysis and utilized the same terms. On the first page of an article entitled "Toward an Ethnosociology of South Asian Caste Systems," Marriott and Inden wrote, "[t]he aims of this chapter are inspired by the results of a cultural style of analysis exemplified in Schneider's book *American Kinship*" (Marriott and Inden 1977: 227). Similarly, in "Hindu Transactions: Diversity without Dualism," Marriott proposed a model of Indian transaction and personhood that specifically referred to Schneider's model (1976: 110). What these authors proposed, however, was a radical opposition between American understandings (Marriott 1976: 110) – or "Western" or "Euro-American" ones (Marriott and Inden 1977: 228) – and those of Indian actors.

Instead of the dual categories of nature and law or substance and code, which Schneider had postulated, Indian thinking displayed a "systematic monism" (Marriott 1976: 109). Here code and substance were inseparable – a point that Marriott emphasized by using the forms "code-substance" or "substance-code" (1976: 110). Bodily substance and code for conduct were not only inseparable, they were also malleable: "Actions enjoined by these embodied codes are thought of as transforming the substances in which they are embodied" (Marriott and Inden 1977: 228). Conduct alters substance, and all interpersonal transactions (for example, sex, sharing of food or water, and coresidence) involve the transfer of the moral and spiritual qualities of those involved. Gift-giving transmits both these qualities of the person from donor to recipient as well as the material matter of the gifts. In other words, there is no radical disjunction between the physical and moral properties of persons, or between body and soul. This of course had profound implications for understandings of personhood and caste, and particularly of the significance of food transactions across caste boundaries. Marriott and Inden thus used "the cognitive nonduality of action and actor, code and substance . . . as a universal axiom for restating, through deduction, what we think we know about caste systems" (Marriott and Inden 1977: 229).

The ethnosociological model has an appealing clarity about it, and it appears to make sense of a wide range of phenomena. But it has also been criticized on a number of counts. The most obvious of these is its tendency to oversystematization (see, for example, Barnard and Good 1984: 178–82; Good 1991: 179–82). Anthony Good (2000) argues that to present these ideas as a consistent and coherent philosophical system is not only misleading in the face of marked divergences between informants and localities, it also omits any sociological account of how such knowledge is deployed in practice, the ways in which it can be used to further particular actors' interests, and the different contexts in which this is done. We thus fail to gain an understanding of the relationship between this kind of ideology and behavior in particular contexts.

Ethnographic data from different areas in South Asia have produced rather different versions of indigenous notions of personhood, including those in which body and "spirit," or blood and "spirit," are separately de-rived (see Barnett 1976; McGilvray 1982). Such data suggest that dualism is not totally absent from Indian thought – a point to which I will return later in this chapter. Even within one area or village, different informants often have divergent views on the quite esoteric subjects under examination in these studies. (Outside the Indian context, the tendency of anthropolo-gists to oversystematize procreation beliefs has been noted by Maurice Bloch [1993] and Philip Thomas [1999] in reference to Madagascar.) One method that seems to produce a remarkable level of consistency is to base analysis on the accounts of rather few informants. A striking example of this kind of ethnography is Daniel's *Fluid Signs* (1984), to which I have already referred. Here the author disarmingly admits to giving "not an exhaustive study of the topic of sexual intercourse and procreation, but one man's perspective" (Daniel 1984: 165). I would not, however, dismiss Daniel's account for that reason; many anthropologists do no more but admit rather less.

Most serious of all, perhaps, is the degree of difference proposed in this model between Indian and American, or as it tends to be glossed, between Indian and Western categories. This radical opposition suggests limits to the comparability of ideas about the person between India and the West. On this count, Good (2000) suggests that the ethnosociological model represents an extreme form of orientalism. In an illuminating article on the body in India, Jonathan Parry (1989) has made a number of key points about the contrast proposed between Western dualism and Indian monism. The monist view is one in which body and soul are merged, and persons are not discrete, bounded individuals composed of immutable substance as they are in the West, but instead are "divisible" and constantly changing. As Marriott writes:

Actors and actions, as matters of both natural and moral fact, are thought to be of infinitely varied and unstable kinds, since circulations and combinations of particles of substance-code are continuously occurring (Marriott 1976: 112).

Parry points out, first, that these notions of personhood do "not altogether accord with the quite robust and stable sense of self" (Parry 1989: 494) of his own acquaintances, and second, that it is difficult to see how they would square with the notion of equivalence of members of the same caste:

How, one wonders, could such equivalence be sustained in a world in which *each* actor's substance-code is endlessly modified and transformed by the myriad exchanges in which he is uniquely involved: How, indeed, could anybody ever decide with whom, and on what terms, to interact? (Parry 1989: 494, original italics).

In fact, some of Parry's own work on priests in Benares (e.g. Parry 1980, 1985) suggests that people contemplate such problems with considerable anxiety. Noting the very radical implications of such a contrast in ideas about the person between the West and India, Parry proposes a more complex model in which the kind of ideas documented by the ethnosociologists coexist with another strand of thought more familiar to Westerners – one in which a degree of dualism can be discerned. He also notes that Western ideology is not as thoroughly dualistic as the ethnosociologists have assumed. He suggests, in other words, that both monism and dualism are present in the West and in India, and that to miss this point is also to miss the role of monist ideas as an ideological buttress to caste ranking in India.

These points are all highly pertinent to my discussion here. But before leaving India, I want to return for a moment to the term *substance*. In the second edition of *American Kinship*, Schneider explicitly commented on the use of the opposition between substance and code outside the American context. He stated unequivocally:

I myself make only one limited claim for this opposition; it is an important part of American culture. I make no claims for its universality, generality, or applicability anywhere else (Schneider 1980: 120).

If we compare the use of these terms by Indianist anthropologists, with the original use made of them by Schneider, we are confronted with some striking anomalies. While Marriott insisted on the hyphenated form *substance-code* to underline a contrast with the West, other writers in the same tradition simply used the term *substance* while still emphasizing the same contrast (see, for example, Daniel 1984). There is something rather odd, however, in using one term to refer to two explicitly opposed sets of meanings. Schneider, as we saw, had argued that blood or natural substance was unalterable and indissoluble in the context of American kinship. In India, it was precisely the mutability, fluidity, and transformability of substance that underlay a contrasting set of notions about the person, and relations between persons (see Daniel 1984: 2–3). There were, however, differences in the way *substance* was deployed even within a small group of seemingly like-minded scholars of South Asia (cf. Östör, Fruzetti, and Barnett 1982).

To sum up, in the comparison of the West with India, different understandings of *substance* were being posited as underlying quite different notions of the person. A clear understanding of the analytic significance of using this term was therefore crucial. The problem with *substance* lay partly in the opposition to code for conduct, which Schneider had used in his analysis of American data. Following Parry's argument, we might say that the strong demarcation between these two orders fits neither the Indian nor the Western cases. But another problematic aspect of using this term arose from quite a different source: the multiple meanings of *substance* in English, which I referred to at the beginning of this chapter. *Substance*, as we saw, can denote a separate thing (such as a person or a body part); it can denote a vital part or essence of that thing or person; and it can also denote corporeal matter more generally, the tissue or fluid of which bodies are composed. This conflation becomes particularly critical when it is precisely the relation between persons – the discreteness or relative permeability of persons, the flows of bodily fluids, the exchanges of corporeal matter – that is at issue. Where one term can mean the discrete thing, its essence, and the matter of which it is composed, the use of that term as an analytic category is, at the very least, likely to be a confusing basis for achieving a comparative understanding of the relations among personhood, essences, and bodily matter.

Substance in Melanesia

These issues are at the heart of analyses of kinship in terms of substance in Melanesia. Significantly, the migration of substance as an analytic category to Melanesia was roughly contemporaneous with its appearance in studies of India. But although the Indianists who I have cited referred directly to Schneider's work on American kinship, they made no mention of Melanesian studies. Later commentators, however, have noted the connection. Arjun Appadurai suggests that Marriott's rendering of Indian ideas "looks more Melanesian, than say, Chinese" (Appadurai 1988: 755, cited in Spencer 1995). In contrast, the examples I will cite from Melanesia make more explicit reference to understandings of substance in India than to Schneider's use of *substance* versus *code*.

Before examining Melanesian substance in detail, it may be helpful to signal in advance the direction of my argument. In tracing the passage of *substance* from America to India, and from there to Melanesia, I am struck by how the same term takes on quite different meanings. In the Melanesian case, not only is the reference of *substance* to *code*, which was central to Schneider's depiction of *American Kinship* and which retains a presence in the analyses of India, dropped, but *substance* itself is described as something that is *inherently* transmissible and malleable.

In American kinship, Schneider had emphasized the immutability of *substance* as well as its distinction from *code*. In India it was the inseparability of *substance* and *code* that apparently conferred malleability. In Melanesia, in the examples I cite, what is emphasized is the "analogizing" capacity of *substance* – the way it can be substituted by detachable "things," such as meat, women, or pearl shells. Considerably influenced by depictions of personhood and substance in India, and in direct contrast with America, what is *not* malleable (that is, not analogized in a range of other substances) and *not* transmitted comes to be described in Melanesia as *by definition* not substance. As we shall see, however, some of the analytic moves in the development of this argument are more explicit than others.

Strathern's comparative analysis of Melanesian relationships and substance in *The Gender of the Gift* (1988) explicitly draws on Marriott's model of the "dividual" person (Strathern 1988: 13), but her approach is also strongly influenced by the earlier work of anthropologists such as Roy Wagner (Wagner 1977; Strathern 1988: 278). Strathern cites the following passage from Marriott as "pertinent":

Persons – single actors – are not thought in South Asia to be "individual," that is, indivisible, bounded units, as they are in much of Western social and psychological theory as well as in common sense. Instead, it appears that persons are generally thought by South Asians to be "dividual" or divisible. To exist, dividual persons absorb heterogeneous material influences. They must also give out from themselves particles of their own coded substances – essences, residues, or other active influences – that may then reproduce in others something of the nature of the persons in whom they have originated (Marriott 1976: 111, cited in Strathern 1988: 348).

While others have concentrated on the contrast that Strathern draws between Melanesian and Western personhood, gender, and society (see, for example, Cecilia Busby 1997b), I want to focus particularly on aspects of her analysis of substance. The pertinent quote from Marriott provides a useful starting point. Like Wagner before her, Strathern is concerned with flows of substance between people, and with the reproductive capacity of substances.

In a chapter on "Forms Which Propagate," Strathern discusses at length the connections made in the Trobriands between a woman and her child, her husband, and her brother (Strathern 1988: 231–40). Anthropologists have long been familiar with the much disputed claim that Trobriand fathers are perceived locally as having no physiological connection with their children. Strathern has gone further in suggesting that Trobriand mothers are also not connected to their children by ties of substance. She argues this in spite of Bronislaw Malinowski's insistence on the Trobriand assertion that "without doubt or reserve . . . the child is of the same substance as its mother" (Malinowski 1929: 3; cited in Strathern 1988: 235). Malinowski quotes the following Trobriand statements: "'The mother feeds the infant in her body. Then, when it comes out, she feeds it with her milk. . . . The mother makes the child out of her blood'" (Malinowski 1929: 3). I am intrigued by such a stark contradiction. How does Strathern come to deny Malinowski's straightforward claim with such force? What work is the idea of substance doing here?

Basing her alternative rendering of the Trobriand material on Annette Weiner's (1976) account, Strathern suggests that a Trobriand woman does not feed the fetus within her:

Blood is simply the counterpart already in the mother of the spirit children who will be brought her by matrilineal ancestral beings; it is not to be thought of as food at all. Malinowski's error, if we can call it that, comes from mistaking form for substance (Strathern 1988: 235).

As we shall see, the relationship between form and substance is crucial to Strathern's argument. Because of the rules governing their appropriate behavior, a Trobriand brother and sister cannot overtly exchange with each other. The sister produces children, the brother produces yams. These, Strathern argues, are "analogically equivalent" items, which "each must make the other yield." The brother has an interest in the production of his sister's children, but since he cannot interact directly with the sister, his yams go to her husband, who then "opens the way" for the entry of the spirit child at conception. In other words, the crucial act of the husband here is the creation of the woman's body as container for the child. Thus the brother's gifts of yams coerce his sister's husband into creating the separation between the mother and child. It is the father's *activity*, rather than his bodily emissions, that have this effect. The "work . . . of molding the fetus . . . gives the child its bodily form, as an extraneous and partible entity" (1988: 236).

The activities of molding the fetus and, after birth, of feeding the child give the child a form that is different from the child's mother's, and in this way separate the child from its mother. The fetus is a "contained entity within the mother . . . herself composed of *dala* blood," and while the father creates its external form, its internal form is *dala* blood, that is, blood of the matrilineal subclan. "Mother and child are thus internal and external homologues for one another" (Strathern 1988: 237). As I understand it, it is this homologous relationship – the fact that substance is neither transformed food, nor has it been *exchanged* – that is at the root of Strathern's assertion that "Trobriand mother and child are not connected through ties of substance" (1988: 237). This is of course a very particular interpretation of the meaning of substance.

The crucial point is that while the child's blood replicates that of the mother and of her brother:

[T]he mother does not "give" this blood to the fetus as though it were food, any more than the brother impregnates his sister or sister and brother exchange gifts between themselves. And only most indirectly does the mother's brother feed it; the feeding is mediated by the sister's husband's vital act as nurturer. It cannot be the case, then, that the fetus is an extension of the mother's bodily tissue and that the mother "makes" it in this sense. (1988: 238).

Strathern suggests that for Trobrianders, the feeding and growing of children are contrasted activities. A Trobriand father feeds food, which is considered a form of mediating wealth, to his child and to his wife, but they do not contribute to internal substance (1988: 251); the mother's brother "grows" yams, partly for his sister, just as the sister "grows" the child. But "since yams and children are 'the same,' the brother's yams cannot be conceptualised as directly feeding the sister's child, for they are analogues of the child" (1988: 239). Thus, in Strathern's account, the growth of the child is a consequence of the relationship between mother and child – it is not mediated by feeding or transmission of substance. One might put this differently, and say that although substance *is* transmitted, this transmission occurs all at once. There is no ongoing *flow* of substance – and this is what limits its generative capacity.

So, to return to the original question, it is worth considering for a moment just why Strathern is suggesting that the Trobriand mother and child are not connected through ties of substance. It would seem that, in this context, substance must have two properties, which can both be linked to Wagner's earlier account. One property of substance is that it is transmitted – and this underlines the link with Wagner's earlier analysis of "substantive flows" between persons; the second is the substitutability or analogizing capacity of substance (Wagner 1977: 624). Trobriand blood is not analogized in a range of other substances, such as milk, semen, and food (as it is elsewhere in Melanesia; see Strathern 1988: 240–60), and this, as I understand it, is what makes it not a substance. The capacity for analogy is linked to a further property of substance: that it gives content to form. Thus she comments on paternal feeding in the Trobriands, "where substance remains on the surface," that is, it is not an inner condition, and "[w]hat is within has no substance" (1988: 251). Once again we are confronted with a play on several meanings of *substance* – corporeal matter, substance as opposed to form, inner essence.

If we look at this last transformation of substance in comparative terms, we can discern some surprising twists. I noted previously that one of the properties of substance that Schneider underlined in *American Kinship* was its immutability. It was the crucial distinction between this version of substance and more malleable Indian versions of bodily substance to which Marriott drew attention by using the term *substance-code* or *coded substances*. Other writers on India, however, were less punctilious in their usages and, perhaps unwittingly, contributed to a general, if largely implicit, view among anthropologists that an *inherent* property of bodily substance was malleability. Thus Strathern's commentary on the Trobriand material, in which what is not transmittable and malleable is not substance, appears to make sense from an Indian point of view.

From the point of view of *American Kinship*, however, in which immutability was seen as a key property of blood, it might be thought surprising that what was not malleable could therefore not be considered as substance. It is also worth noting that, in its passage to Melanesia, the relationship of substance to code seems to have been lost. This was perhaps predictable given the nature of the larger arguments being made about Western versus non-Western categories, which I discuss later in this chapter. One effect of this transmigration however, was that *substance* itself came to encompass an even less specific domain of meaning than Schneider had originally delineated. Strathern's attempt to limit the use of *substance* may perhaps be understood as a way of underlining its local specificity as well as sharpening its analytic power. But it is also worth noting that the emphasis placed on the "analogizing capacity" of substance in Melanesia, and on its flow between persons, or persons and things, suggested that *substance* was *inherently* relational, whereas the dictionary definitions with which I began this chapter do not attribute a relational quality to *substance*. On the contrary, they refer to something more or less material within which qualities or essences are located.

Melanesian and Indian Substance and Personhood Compared

Strathern's discussion of notions of substance is part of wider analysis of gender and personhood in Melanesia. The model she proposes is broadly comparative: In Melanesia, persons are "partible" or "dividual," in contrast to the individuality of Western personhood. Partible persons are composite mosaics, composed of elements of female and male substance. Gender has to be performed and elicited rather than, as in Western notions, being an inherent property of personhood.

Busby (1997b) has provided an incisive comparison of these ideas with Indian ones based on her own fieldwork in Kerala. In spite of some obvious similarities, Busby notes important divergences between the South Indian and Melanesian cases. Briefly, she suggests that instead of being partible persons, composed of elements of male or female substance, persons in Kerala are permeable and connected. I will explain her contrast between permeable and partible persons shortly. Here gender is essentialized rather than performed or elicited. And it resides, crucially, in what are perceived to be essentially male and female substances – semen and male blood, or womb and breast milk. Thus her informants expressed concerns and anxieties over the proper separation and transmission of these substances, particularly through marriage to the correct category of relative and through the birth of children. Here it is the flow of female substance that connects mothers to their children, and the flow of male substance that connects fathers to their children. Children are related equally to each parent but through a different substantive link; thus the children of two brothers are linked by male substance, and the children of two sisters are linked by female substance. The children of a brother and sister have different male and female substance. This difference is at the heart of the suitability of the cross-cousin as marriage partner.

Busby underlines the distinction between an internally whole person with fluid and permeable body boundaries in South Asia and an internally divided and partible person in Melanesia. In India, substances are transmitted, merge and, within the body, become indistinguishable; bodies cannot be divided according to male and female substantive components. In Melanesia, male and female substances are commonly associated with different parts of the body. Bodies are internally divided into differently gendered parts, and gender is unstable; it must be made known, often in ritual performances (Busby 1997b: 270–1). Thus, in Melanesia, men and women may alternate their perceived gender through specific kinds of transaction with male or female things. In India, by contrast, gender is concerned with bodily essences – men and women can act only in male or female ways respectively – and their activities arise out of bodily differences between men and women.

These distinctions, as Busby points out, are connected to a difference between a focus on relationships in Melanesia and one on persons in South India. Strathern argues that in Melanesia the body "is a microcosm of *relations*" (Strathern 1988: 131; cited in Busby 1997b: 273), whereas in South India the flows of substances between persons "always refer to the persons from whom they originated: they are a manifestation of persons rather than of the relationships they create" (Busby 1997b: 273). Persons are both connected through substantive flows and complete in themselves; they are not microcosms of relations. And here substance itself is differently conceived: "Substance may connect persons in India and in Melanesia, but it is substance as a *flow from* a person compared with substance objectified as part of a person" (1997: 276, original italics).

Clearly, we are not dealing with a simple opposition between Western immutable substance and Melanesian or Indian mutability. It seems that we can discern in all the examples I have discussed elements of immutability and elements of mutability – essences and mixing. Indeed, one might consider these as examples of a kind of cultural speculation on the effects of sedimenting essences, processes of detachment and separation, and the merging and mixing of flows between people. This recalls Parry's (1989) earlier discussion of ideas about the body in India and his emphasis on contrastive strands of thought within both India and the West. In the final section of this chapter, I revisit my own material on Malay bodily substance with such contrastive themes in mind.

Malay Substance

In my own earlier work, I have described discussions I had with Malay people on the island of Langkawi about the relationship between food (particularly rice), breast milk, and blood in the body (Carsten 1995a; 1997: 107–30). Blood has a central place in ideas about life itself and about relatedness. I was told repeatedly that people both are born with blood and also acquire it through life in the form of food, which is transformed into blood in the body. Death occurs when all the blood leaves the body.

Blood is transformed food, as is breast milk. But breast milk is also understood as converted blood, a kind of "white blood." And it has a special power because it is thought to carry emotional as well as physical properties from the mother. Indeed, mothers and their children are thought to be particularly closely connected because a child is fed on the mother's blood in the womb and on her milk after birth. Those who eat the same food together in one house also come to have blood in common, and this is one way in which foster children and affines become connected to those with whom they live.

The status of semen in these ideas about convertibility is somewhat unclear. Some people told me that while the child gets blood from the mother, the father's contribution, the seed, is "just a drop" and less important. In some respects, it seems that semen is seen as another form of white blood, rather like breast milk. In other respects, semen is associated with bone – in particular, the skull, from where it originates, and the backbone, to which it makes its way before conception can occur. In any case, what made a most vivid impression on me in these discussions was the centrality of ideas about blood to the constitution of the body, and to relations of kinship in the broadest sense. I was forever hearing about illnesses in terms of imbalances in the blood, endlessly listening to comments on the effects of different kinds of food on the blood, on the problems of transfusions, on blood pressure, even on the proper color of blood. (My own blood was regarded with approval as being a healthful red.)

One theme that constantly recurred was convertibility. It was not just the conversion of food, milk, and blood that concerned people, but also direct transfers of blood. I have already mentioned a concern about transfusions. Blood groups were also much discussed, and generally blood group O was thought to be particularly good because of its possibilities for transfer. Vampire spirits are a well-known theme in Malay beliefs. Fears about the illicit taking of blood were expressed in stories about one such spirit, Langsuir, who is strongly attracted to postpartum women because of the smell of blood. Murderers, the illicit takers of life, can make themselves invincible by consuming their victim's blood.

As in the Indian and Melanesian cases, Malay ideas about bodily substance can also be linked to personhood. Like corporeal substance, the identity of the Malay person could be said to be partly given at birth and partly acquired through life, along with kin relations, which are also given and acquired. There is also a sense in which Malay personhood can be shown to express both ideas about connectedness and separateness. Connectedness is emphasized in the form of siblingship, which through the existence of spirit siblings predates birth. Ideas about the relative permeability of the body, revealed in discourses about sickness, show considerable concern over the boundaries of the body. The boundedness of individuals is qualified by the strength of bonds between siblings, both spiritual and actual. One might view Malay kinship as partly a series of speculations on the possibilities of boundedness and unboundedness, difference and similarity, between persons. I have described it largely in terms of processes of making similarity.

It should be clear why I could hardly ignore the extensive discourse about blood, and why it seemed tempting to render the Malay word for blood, *darah*, as substance. Substance seemed to capture the centrality of blood to Malay ideas about relatedness. It nicely evoked the idea of blood as a vital essence, necessary for life, as well as the emphasis on mutability between food, blood, and breast milk. Like other anthropologists, I could play on several meanings of substance – content, vital essence, corporeal matter. In truth, until challenged, I didn't think much of the elision of blood and substance. And when challenged, I simply added a note to the effect that this usage seemed in keeping with the force of the Malay ideas I was describing (Carsten 1997: 108).

Nevertheless, it is worth giving further consideration to the suitability of *substance* to convey Malay ideas about blood. The first point I would make is quite simple: I was not translating a Malay term when I used *substance*. I think the same is also likely to be true of other anthropologists who have used the term elsewhere (cf. Thomas 1999). In fact, given the very wide semantic domain of *substance* in English, it seems rather unlikely that we would find an exact equivalent to it in non-European languages.

On the positive side, *substance* apparently captured quite neatly certain qualities of blood in Malay ideas – mutability, transferability, vitality, essence, content. It also captured a tension between the givenness of inherited characteristics and the acquisition of identity through life, which is a central theme in the ideas I was discussing. Blood was partly given at birth, partly acquired and mutable. Crucially, it played a key role in the *transformation* of acquired characteristics into given ones, and vice versa, through the postulated relations between blood, birth, and feeding. Thus blood did not fit neatly into the kind of analytic categories that have been central to the analysis of kinship – the given and the acquired, the biological and the social, substance and code, nature and nurture. In fact, it could be used to destabilize these dichotomies.

Conclusion

It should not be surprising that quite subtle shifts in how the composition of the body is perceived may carry implications for personhood and gender. What is notable in all the literature to which I have referred is that the English term *substance* apparently easily accommodates a remarkable range of indigenous meanings that includes bodily matter, essence, and content in opposition to form, as well as differences in degrees of mutability and fluidity. In this concluding section, I return to the analytic work to which substance has been put – to what substance *does* for kinship.

This work of substance bears some resemblance to the analysis of personhood with which it is so closely connected. I referred at the beginning of the last chapter to Strathern's commentary on the analytic significance of personhood for anthropologists of the 1980s. Personhood, she suggested, had the capacity to "force the reconceptualisation of what we might mean by kinship, so that it fed back into the existing assumptions about kinship, [and] provided a new focus of critique" (Strathern 1997: 8). It drew together "what anthropologists previously distributed in different ways" (1997: 8) – procreation, reproduction, kinship relations.

One might now say something rather similar about substance. Like concepts of the person, substance could be shown to be highly variable in different cultures. The examples I have discussed demonstrate that it was impossible to discuss substance without bringing together a whole range of other themes, including procreation, relations between kin, bodies, personhood, gender, and feeding. Undoubtedly, using *substance* in this way has contributed to a critique of the way that anthropologists have conceived kinship. But there are also some differences between the way that personhood and substance have been analytically deployed. One of these is the degree of explicitness about the analytic status of the terms used. Whereas, as we saw in the previous chapter, the study of the person, from its inception, explicitly distinguished different kinds of personhood analytically (such as the self and the individual), such distinctions have been rather implicit in discussions of *substance*. Indeed, I have tried to show how a blurring of distinctions – for example, between bodily matter, essences, vital parts, and content – was a key element in the fruitfulness of *substance* as an analytic term for opening up the study of persons, bodies, and their relationships.

This blurring has inevitably led to ambiguity, to the obscuring of differences, as well as the opening up of fresh possibilities. I would suggest that it is not the range of meanings itself that has been problematic, rather it is the unexamined nature of this range. In all the non-Western examples I have discussed, we might say that conduct, feeding, living in houses, and growing things in the soil may transform bodily substance. The fruitfulness of *substance* as an analytic term has been partly as a means to express transformability. If we return to the dictionary definitions with which I began this chapter, however, it is notable that the meanings of *substance*, although they include corporeal matter and the consistency of a fluid, do not specify malleability, transformability, or relationality as inherent properties of substance. But these properties have been important aspects of the analytic work achieved by substance in the non-Western examples I have cited.

If in the non-Western examples cited here *substance* has been used to convey meanings that in some respects are more or less the opposite of either its dictionary definition or its use in Schneider's original analysis, this may suggest that it was doing a particular kind of analytic work. The cooption of *substance* to express mutability and transformability, the flow of objects or bodily parts between persons, as well as the capacity to stand for the relations between those persons, suggests a gap in the analytic vocabulary of kinship. The analysis of kinship, in its mid-twentieth century forms, tended to separate and dichotomize the biological and the social domains, nature and nurture, substance and code. But in some non-Western cases, indigenous discourses highlighted processes of conversion, transformation, and flow between the very domains that anthropological analysis distinguished (see Carsten 2000a). *Substance* seemed an appropriate term in descriptions of such processes partly because of the breadth of meanings it encompassed. Simultaneously, *substance* could also be used to destabilize the dichotomizing practices on which the analysis of kinship was based. And this is one way of summing up the way in which substance was deployed in the analysis of Melanesian or Indian material.

But this analytic strategy also involved, as we have seen, setting up another dichotomy – this time not within the terms that defined kinship, but between "the West" and "the rest." Dividual non-Western persons in India or Melanesia could be opposed to the Western individual; substance in India or Melanesia, which was fluid and subject to transformation, could be contrasted to substance in the West, which was permanent and immutable. One purpose of my discussion of personhood and substance in this chapter and the previous one has been to argue against such a stark contrast between Western and non-Western categories. At the beginning of this chapter, I suggested that in the context of kinship in Britain or America, Schneider's original opposition between substance and code seems unnecessarily rigid and restrictive in the light of the material I cited from Edwards, Baumann, and Weston. These examples should encourage us to investigate not just blood as "biogenetic substance," but also the relationship between substance and code, and the degree to which these domains are clearly distinguished and separate; in other words, we need to interrogate closely the combinatory power of substance and code, which according to Schneider was at the heart of the category of "blood" relative.

If the analytic vocabulary of kinship apparently lacked a means to express mutability and relationality in terms of flows between persons or between persons and things, and substance neatly filled that gap, this may have had more to do with the particular history of the academic study of kinship than with European or American folk discourses about kinship. The separation of nature from nurture, the biological from the social, and substance from code was central to a particular juncture in the anthropological analysis of kinship. But it remains to be investigated whether local practices and discourses of kinship in the West privileged the separation of these elements to the same extent, or in the same way, as did the mid-twentieth century academic discourse. At the beginning of the twenty-first century, perhaps those interested in the study of kinship in the West are beginning to see the significance of Schneider's lead and to take seriously the combinatory potential of these elements.

What attracted me about substance as a way to convey Malay ideas about blood was precisely the way it captured the simultaneous boundedness and unboundedness of Malay personhood, and the capacity to transform characteristics that are acquired into those that are given. In these respects, we may conclude that Malay, Indian, Melanesian, and even North American discourses of kinship have a considerable amount in common, while also revealing some quite subtle differences.

SIX

Families into Nation: The Power of Metaphor and the Transformation of Kinship

In the last chapter, I began to examine the distinction between substance and code that is at the heart of David Schneider's analysis of American kinship. It can also be linked to a wider set of oppositions that are quite familiar in the anthropological study of kinship and beyond: the distinction between nature and culture, and between the biological and the social. As we saw, the deployment of these terms in anthropological analysis appears to have carried quite strong implications about the different nature of kinship in the West and "the rest."

Schneider regarded the combinatory potential of substance and code as at the heart of what constituted a blood relative in American ideas (1980: 28). But it is worth pausing for a moment to consider the nature of this combination, and the work that both the separation and the combination of these elements do – both for indigenous ideas about kinship, and for their analysis by anthropologists. In this chapter, I focus on relationships that apparently have no basis in substance, but yet are couched in an idiom of "natural" ties – for example, adoptive ties, "fictive" kinship, and gay kinship. What is the force of casting such relations in a natural idiom? And what tensions are entailed in this kind of work of kinship?

As in previous chapters, I take examples both from Western and non-Western contexts. My aim is to explore further the distinction between substance and code, and to make some comparisons between Western and non-Western cases. By doing so, I hope to illuminate not just the processes of naturalization at work when relationships are cast in an idiom of kinship (see Yanagisako and Delaney 1995), but also the ways in which naturalization itself carries emotional power. This leads me, in the final sections of the chapter, to consider wider metaphorical uses of kinship, and the potential political force of such metaphors. When we examine the links between kinship and nationalism, clearly it is not just in exotic, non-Western contexts that possibilities exist for transforming and creating relations that are cast in an idiom of the natural. Nationalist ideologies, as many have noted, highlight the political salience of the metaphorical uses to which kinship may be put. But what are the mechanisms and slippages that allow kinship to take on these guises? And what gives them their emotional power?

Dissolving the Boundaries: Fostering as Transformation

My starting point for thinking about these topics is, once again, the Malay practices and discourses of kinship that I encountered during my fieldwork on the island of Langkawi in the 1980s. In the last chapter, I discussed the terms in which people described to me ideas about human blood and milk. That these bodily substances are affected by environmental factors – including food, living in one house, emotional encounters, and so on – as well as by birth, is not just of symbolic importance. I have described elsewhere (Carsten 1995a, 1995b, 1997) how ideas about blood and relatedness connect to historical and demographic features of Malay life. The first of these features is substantial demographic mobility, which has historically been central to the settlement of pioneer areas in outlying regions of the Malay states. On an island such as Langkawi, situated on the northern borders of the state of Kedah, it was possible at the end of the nineteenth century and in the early decades of the twentieth to settle and make a living by clearing new land or turning to fishing for gaining a livelihood. The establishment and enlargement of new communities were intricately bound up with the way connections of kinship could be established by in-marriage and by the fostering of new immigrants. In Malay terms, it is generally considered a good thing to marry those who are "close." Such closeness can be perceived in terms of genealogical connection, geographic proximity, social standing, and similarity of features or dispositions. Staying in one house, eating together, fostering, or intermarrying can all set in train processes of gradually becoming similar to those among whom one lives. I have argued (Carsten 1995b, 1997) that, from the point of view of villagers in Langkawi, an ideal guest is one who stays for a long time and eventually settles, marries, and has children on the island.

The second demographic feature, which I see as linked to the ideas about bodily substance I described earlier, is the widespread practice of fostering and the strong tendency to cast relations in this idiom however brief or long their duration. A substantial proportion of village children are brought up in the houses of those who are not their birth parents, or spend at least some period of time in this way. It is very notable that villagers have a strong desire to describe any guest – from a young man brought home for a few days as a friend of an adult son, to visiting students working on projects for a week or so – in the idiom of fostering. Although these kinds of informal fostering arrangements do not generally involve inheriting property from foster parents, as elsewhere in Southeast Asia (see, for example, Janowski 1995; Schrauwers 1999), there is no doubt that the capacity to host foster children conveys prestige. But the effects of these usages are worthy of further comment.

The tendency to blur the distinction between bringing up a grandchild, niece, or nephew over many years and hosting a visiting student for a few days or weeks suggests that the underlying processes involved in these forms of hospitality may potentially be quite similar. The ideal guest reflects back on the ideal hosts: She or he is so overwhelmed by local generosity, and by the welcoming atmosphere, that a short stay lengthens and eventually ceases to be temporary. Those who settle permanently are of course no longer guests; in the process of living with local people, sharing food and house space, and eventually marrying and having children, they have become kin. It is perhaps not surprising that the feeding of visitors, which may be the first stage in a long series of acts of hospitality, often has a coercive edge to it.

Thus what might appear at the beginning as a metaphorical usage of kinship is gradually and imperceptibly transformed into ties of blood and birth. In fact, I would hesitate to use the term *metaphorical* in this context. When talking of foster childen, villagers always emphasize how they are likely to be the favorites of their foster parents. They also describe how a foster child who lives with foster relatives for a long time will gradually come to resemble them in appearance and manner – indeed, changes to my own appearance were often commented upon with approval in this regard. If food is gradually transformed into blood in the body, and those who live together come to resemble each other as well as develop emotional closeness, then in the long term this is surely a quite literal process of creating kinship.

Similar processes, in which physical and social aspects of kinship apparently merge into each other, can be discerned in cases of fostering or adoption outside Southeast Asia. Mary Weismantel (1995) describes how in the highland Ecuadorean community of Zumbagua a high proportion of kin are adopted. Adoption here is neither rare nor a last resort. As in the Malaysian case, there is a local emphasis on feeding in the creation of kinship – "the Zumbagua family consists of those who eat together," and "the hearth . . . supplants the marriage bed as the symbol of conjugal living and the bond of blood as the emblem of parenthood" (Weismantel 1988: 169; cited in Weismantel 1995: 693). Once again, because flesh is locally conceived as formed from food, bodies and substance become linked through prolonged feeding. And so, over time, those who live and eat together come to share flesh and to resemble each other physically.

In this context, Weismantel emphasizes that adoptive kinship can hardly be considered "fictive" in the classic anthropological sense. In fact, she draws a contrast between the shocked reaction of a nonlocal nurse when a child's adoption is spoken about in that child's presence, and Zumbagua attitudes, which do not in any way attempt to hide from children the facts of adoptive kinship. Local practices thus do not appear to privilege biological kinship. In Zumbagua, she argues, nature cannot be regarded as having primacy over culture (1995: 690–1). But instead of merely reversing the prioritization of biological aspects of kinship over the social in the analysis of kinship, Weismantel stresses that feeding itself is a process that combines physiological and social aspects (see also Carsten 1995a, 1997).

Feeding, which is at once a biological, symbolic, and social process, creates what Weismantel calls "material links" between people (1995: 694). But because this kind of feeding occurs over time, rather than at a particular moment, as in Western ideas about conception, it carries the implication that kinship is gradually created rather than originating in a single moment of sexual procreation, as it apparently does in the Western case. Weismantel's argument is conceived as a critique of a symbolic approach to kinship, and aims to use Zumbagua kinship practices as a means to get beyond the materialist/symbolic, or the biological/cultural, divide in the analysis of kinship. And yet, as Susan McKinnon (1995) has commented, her argument sometimes relies on, and appears to reiterate, these very dichotomies. If McKinnon is right to point out that Weismantel's project has much in common with the approach she seeks to undermine, this draws our attention to the difficulties of escaping the terms in which much of the anthropological analysis of kinship has been put.

The Malaysian and the Ecuadorean cases are suggestive, I think, in that they help us to problematize the distinction between what is biological and what is cultural, and it is significant that they do this in very similar ways. In neither the Langkawi nor the Zumabagua example is fostering statistically uncommon, and hence an exemplar of the primacy of biological kinship, as suggested in the classic anthropological accounts. Adoptive kinship in these communities does not simply serve as an arena in which "fictive" kinship can be distinguished from a backdrop of "real" – that is, biologically based – ties and hence reinforce the latter's primacy (see Malinowski 1930: 137; Schneider 1984: 171). Instead of being a vehicle for distinguishing the social from the biological, fostering appears to be a means of transforming the former into the latter, or of merging one into the other.

In both Zumbagua and Langkawi, the link between what is social and what is biological in kinship is provided by the consumption of food and its transformation in the body. The permeability of the boundary between what might be considered social and what is biological in these two very different non-Western contexts urges me to look again at the deployment of these terms in specific Western examples.

Unraveling the Fiction

Schneider suggested that the fundamental and implicit assumption, on which the entire analysis of kinship from Henry Maine and Lewis Henry Morgan to Meyer Fortes and Claude Lévi-Strauss rested, was that "blood is thicker than water." Kinship was what Schneider called "a privileged system" because it derived from the bonds of sexual procreation, and this was seen as a natural and biological process, whatever cultural value this process might be accorded (1984: 155–77). It followed that adoption had a particular importance in the classic accounts precisely because it afforded an opportunity to observe the apparently universal distinction between kin relations that are "true" or "real," that is, biologically based, and those that are "fictive," that is, those that do not derive from ties of sexual procreation (1984: 171–3).[1] The Malay and Ecuadorean examples

---

[1] I am grateful to Michael Lambek for drawing my attention to the fact that "fictive" does not necessarily imply "made up" or "untrue" but can mean simply to fashion or to make. Nevertheless, as Schneider's discussion of adoption makes clear, it was precisely in the former sense of relations that were not natural or intrinsic, and therefore not "true" or "real" because they were not derived from ties of sexual procreation, that adoption was considered a fiction in the kinship theories of Maine, Bronislaw Malinowski, W. H. R. Rivers, Lévi-Strauss, and others.

are important not because they suggest that people in these communities are not capable of making such a distinction – which they no doubt are – but rather that these cultures place emphasis elsewhere. If the process of transforming social ties of neighborhood into those of blood is central to Malay kinship, then drawing distinctions between "real" and "fictive" ties is quite antithetical to Malay kinship.

For Schneider, it was clear that the analytical assumptions to which I have referred were not just implicit but they were themselves derived from European culture (1984: 175). For this reason, I want to look closely at some examples taken from Europe and North America, where we might expect the separation between "real" and "fictive" ties to be quite clear and unambiguous. I want to take up again two cases to which I referred briefly in Chapter 5. The first is Gerd Baumann's description of ethnically plural Southall in London, where there is a widespread recourse to an idiom of "cousinhood" among Sikh, Hindu, Muslim, Afro-Caribbean, and White youth. Baumann's ethnography pays close attention to the difficulty of according genealogical specificity to these claims, and to the method-ological problems that this causes for anthropologists with an interest in kinship (Baumann 1995: 727–30). What is important is that "the empha-sis on cousins observable among Southall youth is shared across locally salient ethnic, religious and cultural boundaries" (1995: 729). Baumann demonstrates that although cousin claims differ according to the different kinship patterns and migration histories of these groups, their salience derives from the same source. This is precisely the fusion of Schneider's two orders of kinship – that of nature and of law. What cousins do for Southall youth is encapsulated in the phrase "cousins are friends who are kin and kin who are friends" (1995: 734). Cousins, in other words, invoke both the obligations of kinship and the choice of friendship, both the trust and loyalty that derive from kinship and the personal prefer-ence characteristic of friendship. Thus young people invoke cousinship in particular kinds of contexts – for example, when trying to get permis-sion from parents to go out with others, or as a potential threat when defending oneself from bullying by others, or when trying to excuse one's own deviant behavior. Baumann makes clear how such invocations are efficacious precisely because they simultaneously draw on the morality of both kinship and friendship.

It is significant, however, that claims of cousinhood are always made within one's religious "community" – unlike ties of friendship, which commonly cross religious or locally perceived "ethnic" boundaries. Baumann notes that this structural opposition between cousin claims and ties of friendship entails a paradox. Kinship is, after all, the realm of ties that are given rather than made:

That it is a kinship term which affords this counter-balance to "mixing with all" and "having friends from other cultures" is worth noting. Kinship, and by implication kinship bonds among peers, represent the epitome, to most Southall youth, of bonds beyond question. Kinship, or simply "family" or "blood," provides the one discursive realm that stands for axiomatic certainty. Much of the social world may be characterized by fashion and change, by rules with exceptions and contingencies without rules. Amidst this universe of cultural relativity, kinship represents that which is paradigmatically real, given and natural (Baumann 1995: 736).

As Baumann notes, although Southall youth view kinship as paradigmatically natural, they simultaneously view the different locally found marriage and kinship patterns – for example, between Afro-Caribbeans and Asian Muslims – as "part of their culture" (1995: 736). Here culture and nature are not two opposed orders, but culture itself is naturalized as part of nature, or as one informant succinctly put it, "it's natural to do what your culture tells you to do" (1995: 737).

Baumann suggests that this naturalization of culture, and the fusion of nature and choice, may be the source of the power of cousin claims:

Humans are produced, and thus given kin, in the same way the world over, and a cousin is a cousin is a cousin. It is perhaps this apparent certainty of kinship as a real thing, the same across "cultures" and their "communities," that makes the cousin such a powerful, and seemingly unquestionable, trope among peers of disparate backgrounds (1995: 737).

If cousin claims are powerful precisely because they merge what is given and what is made, or Schneider's order of nature and order of law, then how are we to view the "fiction" behind such claims to kinship? As in the Malaysian and Ecuadorean cases, it is apparent that merging rather than distinguishing the "real" and the "fictive" (in the sense of classical kinship theory) is what gives these kinship ties their salience. Lest it be thought that this fusion is in some way particularly connected to the exigencies of life in multicultural Southall, I want now to recall another example to which I briefly referred in Chapter 5 – that of gay kinship in North America as described by Kath Weston (1991, 1995).

Weston's depiction of formal kinship ideology among gays and lesbians in San Francisco in the 1980s makes clear that what makes kinship "real" or authentic in this context is not biogenetic connection but duration in time. In the construction of an alternative ideology of the family, there is an explicit refusal to accept biological connectedness as the source of of kinship. Instead, the construction of an apparent oxymoron, "chosen families," rests on permanence as the source, and simultaneously the proof, of the authenticity of these ties. Weston describes the diverse forms that such families may take and the many households that they encompass, including ex-lovers, gay and heterosexual friends, children who may or may not be biogenetically connected to those who have supplied parental care, and networks of those who care for those requiring support through illness – especially AIDS (Weston 1995: 93). Permanence is here not simply ascribed as a natural quality of blood ties, as in the dominant ideology of kinship, but must be actively produced in time (1995: 90–1, 99–102).

Weston notes that the refusal to accept an equation between "biological" connection and permanence can be read as an explicit rejection of dominant heterosexual kinship ideology. But the construction of an idiom of "chosen families" based on endurance through time can also be seen as a move that assimilates gay relationships to the dominant mode. By highlighting the subtle shifts in meaning entailed by ideas about permanence, she shows that in fact neither depiction is adequate. As she points out, although the equation between "natural" ties and permanence is commonly made in discourses of kinship, the attribution of permanence to the biological processes of sexual procreation, birth, life, and death is in any case quite arbitrary:

From mortality and procreation to the perpetual renewal of tissue at the cellular level, biological processes might just as easily constitute a signifier of change and flux rather than continuity and control (Weston 1995: 103).

Although the invocation of endurance through time might be seen as a restatement of the dominant kinship discourse, Weston argues that this move represents neither a radical alternative strategy nor an assimilation to the dominant mode. This is because the meaning of enduring solidarity itself shifted in response to the struggle to claim legitimacy for gay kinship in the particular material and historical conditions of American life in the 1980s. Here permanence becomes not an inherent feature of certain kinds of relationships, but must be produced through sustained attention and effort (1995: 102–6).

I will have more to say about the equation of biological ties with permanence in the following section. But first I want to consider what this North American case tells us about the separation of "natural" and "social" aspects of kinship, and the depiction of "fictive" ties in anthropological analysis. Once again we seem to be confronted by evidence of an explicit emphasis on the creation of kinship – this time through care and work. It is the sustained effort involved in maintaining relationships over time that both produces chosen families and proves their authenticity. If, as Weston argues, these attitudes are neither a straightforward rejection nor a simple reproduction of dominant modes of kinship, then this perhaps suggests that the symbolic work of kinship leaves much more open than Schneider's analysis implies. Here the connection between biological procreation and naturally enduring ties is broken, while friendships connote stability and permanence. But, as Weston shows, to categorize such friendships as "fictive" kinship, in opposition to the "true" relations derived from sexual procreation, runs counter to gay kinship accounts in which such friendships are portrayed as "'just as real' as other forms of kinship" (1995: 99).

To assert the primacy of biogenetic connectedness in this context would appear at the very least to ignore what the native informants are telling us about their explicit ideology of kinship. And this places the authorship of the "fiction" of fictive kinship in some doubt. If, in this case, what anthropologists have been used to describing as "fictive" kinship is asserted to be just as real as "true" kinship, or if, in the Southall case, it is virtually impossible to establish the genealogical basis of cousin claims, then whose fiction is it? Schneider asserted that the primacy of biological ties in anthropological analyses of kinship arose from indigenous European and American folk assumptions. But it would appear that not all the natives adhere to these assumptions in the same way or to the same degree. And this might suggest that the primacy of biology was a product of a particular analytic strategy rather than straightforwardly imported from European folk models of kinship.

Adoption Reunions

In 1997, when I began conducting a series of interviews in Scotland with those who had been involved in reunions between adults adopted as children and their birth kin, it was with a specific idea in mind. My hunch was that accounts of these reunions might offer a convenient handle on some of the ways in which "biological" and "social" kinship are separated in contemporary Britain. Such reunions, I surmised, would necessarily be predicated upon quite sharp juxtapositions and articulations between what is expected from, or attributed to, adoptive as opposed to birth kin. My own hesitancy about the research I was undertaking was well articulated for me by a colleague who prefaced her friendly enquiries about this work with the remark, "Oh, are they all terribly geneticist?" Indeed, the assumption that the motivations of adopted people seeking such meetings would reveal thoroughly "geneticist" views about kinship and personhood was a depressingly obvious one to make. The reality, which I am just beginning to tease apart, is of course somewhat different.

In the interviews that I conducted, a number of apparently typical scenarios emerged. In Chapter 4 I discussed how the most frequent response to being asked what had prompted interviewees to search for their birth kin was simply, "to know where I came from," "to be complete," or "to find out who I am." Indeed, the answers I got were so formulaic that they suggested that the question itself was almost redundant – wasn't it entirely obvious why one would want to undergo this process? I also alluded in Chapter 4 to the considerable pain and upheaval that the experience of searching for and then meeting with birth kin often involved. Very often, I sensed that this pain had begun a long time before the actual search was initiated. Relations with adoptive kin were described to me in very variable ways by different informants. In some cases, adoptive parents were described in highly positive terms as being extremely loving and supportive, so much so that they were sometimes felt to have been almost too protective or indulgent. In others, these relations were clearly tense and problematic or were experienced as rather distant and quite unaffectionate. Whatever the nature of these ties, the longing to connect to one's birth relatives seemed almost axiomatic. In just one or two cases, interviewees themselves expressed some surprise that they had undergone this process – "it was nothing that really concerned me" – but then they simply attributed this presumption elsewhere – to friends or others who expressed interest and concern.

All of those whom I interviewed vividly described their anxiety and nervousness as they neared the end of their search and attempted to set up an initial meeting – usually with a birth mother. In one terribly poignant case, a young married woman with her own family recalled how she had gone to the lengths of buying a new outfit, and how carefully she had calculated her desired appearance:

I'd just been out and I'd bought myself a new jumper. I thought I'll wear my trouser suit and this new jumper to meet her. I had it all planned out – I didn't want to look too dressy, I didn't want to look too scruffy. I just wanted to look in between, because I had this idea that maybe she was quite poor. . . .

The importance of making the right kind of initial appearance is vividly conveyed here – as is the potential for disjunctions of wealth or class. But as her search came to its conclusion, this woman discovered that her mother (who, it transpired, had herself made repeated but unsuccessful attempts to contact her daughter) had died not long before her daughter discovered her identity. Death was in fact a surprisingly recurrent theme in the narratives I collected. Very frequently, it turned out that a birth mother or a birth father was no longer living, and this was often the most traumatic of many difficult discoveries.[2]

The outcome of these searches was entirely unpredictable. When I asked them what advice they would pass on to others who were considering undertaking a search for birth kin, interviewees inevitably reiterated this uncertainty over what might be discovered about their backgrounds. "I would say go for it – so long as they know what they want out of it, and be ready for the downsides of it. Always prepare yourself for the downsides of it." In just a few cases, my informants described being able

---

[2] Elsewhere (Carsten 2000b) I explore the consequences of adoption reunions in terms of tracing temporal continuities in adoptees' lives, and suggest that part of the emotional upheaval of an adoptee discovering that a birth parent had died before the parent and child had been able to meet might be attributable to a kind of foreclosing of possibilities – both in terms of relations that might actually be established and the imaginative space for fantasizing about the future of such relationships.

to establish some kind of harmonious relations with his or her birth kin. And it was striking that such positive outcomes tended to occur in cases where relations between the adopted person and his or her adoptive parents were also clearly warm and harmonious. Even here, meetings between birth kin tended to be conducted on a somewhat infrequent and quite formal basis. In the great majority of cases, however, these relations seemed to have a doomed quality about them. They were as impossible to establish now as they had been in the past – doubly foreclosed, as it were – by death, by particular histories, by the nature of the personalities involved, by the excess of demands on one side or on both. One woman described to me how, not long after an initial meeting, her birth mother had started to make demands and give advice in a way that she felt was quite unwarranted. As she put it, her birth mother simply didn't have that right; she had forfeited it when she had given up her daughter for adoption thirty years before. Several interviewees expressed the idea that the normal exchanges of kinship are not an automatic right, but a privilege that is earned through the demonstrated hard effort that goes into nurturing and caring for a child. As one adoptee told me, "I wasn't after another mother; I have one." Such statements were in part a kind of declaration of loyalty to adoptive parents, but they also expressed some of the tensions involved in establishing a new set of relations with birth kin.

The acknowledged importance of time and effort to the production of kinship (see also Modell 1994), and a strong disavowal that in the absence of such sustained nurturance there is an automatic bond of kinship given by the facts of birth, might be thought surprising in people who had committed considerable time and effort to discovering whom their birth relatives were. But it recalls the statements about chosen families in America that I cited earlier. In the case of gay kinship, time and endurance, rather than being an inherent feature of relations ascribed by birth, are both the basis and the proof of "proper" – that is, "created" – kinship. While the act of seeking out birth relatives appears in a very obvious sense to underline the primacy of birth ties in the culture of British kinship, in other ways these adopted people simultaneously disturb that primacy. In questioning the rights of birth parents, as well as in the frequent acknowledgments of the role that their own adoptive parents have played, interviewees strongly assert the values of care and effort that go into the creation of kin ties.

As in the case of gay kinship, this "interference" to the symbolic value of birth ties is accompanied by shifts in the value given to time itself in the production of kinship. A striking feature of many of the interviews I conducted was the frequent recourse made to visual artifacts of various kinds – letters, photographs, poems, official documents, and articles of babies' clothing – that were either produced or referred to in the course of conversation. Where *birth* does not imply certainty, endurance, or solidarity, it is emptied of most of the symbolic meaning it has in the dominant discourse of kinship, and time itself has a key role in producing new meanings for kinship. The visual artifacts that were regularly produced for my inspection were a literal production of history. Like objects in a museum, they gave historical depth to current versions of the identities of those whom I interviewed. The significance of these objects and the kind of retrospective history being constructed was considerably heightened by the frequency with which not only adoption but the death of a birth parent had disrupted the flow of time in these relationships. Whether such deaths preceded or followed the discovery of a birth parent's identity, they encapsulated the very considerable dislocations of "kinship time" experienced by those seeking reunions.

If the motivations of those seeking reunions were in some way to discover "where they had come from," then the importance of constructing a documented history with its accompanying mnemonic objects is not hard to grasp. But the assumption that these searches were predicated on a thoroughly geneticist view of human nature or personhood was not borne out. And here there is perhaps a divergence from the American case where Kaja Finkler (2000) suggests that adoptees' searches for their birth kin are premised upon a quite thoroughly geneticized view of their health status, personalities, and kinship (Finkler 2000: 121–2).[3]

In Chapter 4 I described how one interviewee had felt it necessary to establish the identity of her birth father by DNA testing, in spite of her own appraisal of his character as quite dishonest, and of the manifest impossibility of establishing a satisfactory relationship with him. The results of such a test would establish the truth – or as she put it, "stop the lies" – in the face of his persistent evasions, but clearly she would not by this stage have asserted very much beyond this physical tie to her birth father. Interviewees often talked about aspects of their own physical appearance in relation to that of their adoptive and their birth parents. One woman described how, as a child, she had always been very much aware of her curly hair because her adopted parents and their families had straight hair. When she eventually met her birth mother, she realized the provenance of her curls. But in this case, as in many others, the relationship itself had not got onto a harmonious footing. While physical connections were often easy to make, emotional ties did not necessarily follow.

In another case, a young man vividly described the acute misery he had felt growing up as the only black child in his neighborhood and school. But when in his thirties he managed to trace his birth mother (who was white) and finally met her, although "it was a good feeling of meeting her," he described how the woman he faced was a "total stranger" – there was simply no connection:

There's definitely no "ting," connection, like that, because this is somebody you don't know. You don't know this person, it's a total stranger. It might not have been my mother, she could have sent somebody else.

This lack of any connection was reiterated in many interviewees' accounts of their first meeting with birth kin, and contrasts sharply with

---

[3] Finkler's informants, however, often appear to be quite equivocal on this point (see, for example, Finkler, 2000: 131, 135, 141–3, 151, 154, 162, 170).

media accounts of reunions, which tend to be cast in highly romantic and sentimental tones. These ties too required time – as a necessary but not sufficient input – to establish themselves. A few of those I interviewed did feel some initial sense of connectedness, but they were a minority. Nor did reunions with different birth relatives necessarily take the same course. The young man who denied any sense of connectedness with his birth mother not only established a good relationship with his maternal half sister, but also came to know quite a lot about his birth father, who had died shortly before his son discovered his identity. In the absence of any possibility of meeting, it was clear that the facts he had established about his father's identity had not only assured him of his own connection to this man, but had been instrumental in resolving his own uncertainties over "where he had come from."

When I asked those whom I interviewed how they viewed the relative importance of "nature" and "nurture" in their own personal make-up, the responses were very variable. Most simply said, quite unremarkably, that they thought their personalities were a result of a mixture of both their genetic inheritance and the environment in which they had grown up, although some responses attributed the greater role to biology or to environment. One woman told me that her adoptive parents had never seemed anything like her: "it's like living in a house of people who are aliens." Some said that although meeting a birth parent had made sense of a particular character trait or a talent that they possessed, they felt their overall personalities and the course their life had taken had been shaped more by the way they had been brought up. My hunch is that such statements probably would not differ sharply, either in their content or their variation, from those of the general population.

What then to make of the separation of "biological" and "social" aspects in these accounts of kinship? My overwhelming impression is that this distinction is rather more muddled than any simple model would lead us to expect. Here birth does not imply "diffuse enduring solidarity," emptied as it is of the connection to certainty, longevity, or obligations and rights. Adoptive kinship, meanwhile, from the point of view of the child, is stripped of the elements of choice or preference that anthropologists generally attribute to friendship or "fictive kinship." In trying to establish new relations with birth kin, adopted people must refashion the symbols of kinship. The ways in which they do so do not suggest the heavy reliance on a genetic content of kinship, as we might expect. The symbolic importance of birth ties, which is apparently reiterated by the process of searching for birth kin, is in many cases disrupted or denied in the troubled outcomes of these searches. Nor can we perceive a very sharp or consistent distinction made between what "travels in the blood" and what is absorbed from the environment. Instead there appears to be a considerable degree of picking and choosing, or what Jeannette Edwards and Marilyn Strathern (2000) term "interdigitation," between the superfluity of elements of kinship that are available. Schneider's two opposed orders of nature and law become almost inextricably intertwined when letters or legal documents can stand in for blood or nurturance, or an informant asserts that a birth mother felt like "a total stranger." The suggestion that indigenous folk models of Western kinship were the source of the overwhelming symbolic power attributed by anthropologists to sexual procreation is likewise put into question when time, care, and sustained effort take their place beside birth in the culture of kinship.

From Substance to Metaphor?

The material I have cited so far suggests that the symbolic potential of kinship in Britain and North America is to a considerable extent open to creative reformulations. Indeed, although anthropologists tend, either implicitly or explicitly, to juxtapose Western kinship to that of the non-Western societies they study, the cases I have discussed here appear to have quite a lot in common. Without wishing to minimize important differences in the social contexts and history of the particular communities or people studied in Malaysia, San Francisco, Southall, Ecuador, or Scotland, one cannot help but note a rather obvious similarity in the susceptibility of kinship to continuous transformations and adaptations. It is these creative possibilities that lend kinship its very great symbolic force – a power that is all the more salient because it emanates from the emotional and practical circumstances of people's everyday lives – from the things they hold most dear, and with which they are, in every sense, most familiar. This symbolic force makes the implications of anthropologists' and sociologists' attempts to divide Western and non-Western societies on the basis of their kinship quite crucial.

In arguing that kinship in the West has a fundamentally private significance while in non-Western societies it is constitutive of the public, political order, we foreclose the possibility of understanding the ways in which kinship can become a powerful political symbol. Such symbols appeal to the emotions of ordinary citizens just as strongly in Britain or Bosnia as they do in America, India, or Israel.

An example of what I have in mind here is provided by Iris Jean-Klein's (2000, 2001) subtle and illuminating account of the explicit politicization of everyday domestic processes, such as visiting, eating, and celebrating marriages, during the Palestinian Intifada. Jean-Klein traces the myriad links between such everyday processes and an emergent nation-state, documenting the production of new "moral selves" by young men, their mothers, and sisters that involve new practices of gender and kinship.

In a short article first published in 1969, Schneider (1977) argued very forcefully that, far from being separate domains, kinship, religion, and nationality in American culture were structured by the same terms, and that the boundaries between them were blurred: "all of the symbols of American kinship seem to 'say' one thing: they provide for relationships of diffuse, enduring solidarity" (1977: 67). Schneider noted the parallels between the two principal ways one can be a citizen – by birth or by "naturalization," that is, a legal process – and the two ways one can be a relative – in nature or in law. He suggested that, just as in kinship the two elements of nature and of law give rise to three categories of being a relative (by birth, by law, and by a combination of the two), so the same is true of citizenship. One can be an American by birth but take up another citizenship by naturalization, one can become an American through naturalization, and one can be born an American and be one by law.

Schneider was particularly concerned with the implications of what he saw as the identical structuring of nationality, kinship, and religion for putting together "a useful definition of kinship" (1977: 68). My concern here is somewhat different. It is to consider for a moment the crucial question raised (but not answered) by Benedict Anderson (1983: 16) about nationalism: Why is it that the nation exercises such an extraordinary emotional appeal over its citizens? Why, in other words, are people prepared to lay down their lives for their country? But I want to take the less trodden route of approaching this question via kinship instead of via politics.[4] Rather than simply assuming that the connection between family and nation is a metaphorical one, I think it is worth scrutinizing the "blurred boundaries" between kinship, the nation, and religion more carefully.[5]

Carol Delaney (1995) suggests that, in the case of modern Turkey, the same procreative imagery is at work in religion, kinship, and the ideology of the nation-state, and that this is a prime source of the naturalization of gender hierarchies. The nation-state is inherently gendered – by "fixing the boundaries of the motherland," in other words, ensuring the state's integrity and virtue (1995: 186). By constituting Kemal Ataturk as "father of the nation" in the 1920s, the ideology of modern Turkey drew on

---

[4] Anderson himself suggests the fruitfulness of treating nationalism "as if it belonged with 'kinship' and 'religion,' rather than with 'liberalism' or 'fascism'" (1983: 15).

[5] See also Michael Herzfeld (1987, 1997) on the way that nationalism expands on locally conceived "natural" relations of kinship. This expansion can in turn be further enlarged. Thus Liisa Malkki (1994) discusses how imagining the nation necessitates "the imagining of an international community, a 'Family of Nations.'" In this way, internationalism naturalizes nationalism (1994: 62).

a procreative and gendered imagery already inscribed in religious and familial domains:

> *Vatandas*, the word coined to mean "citizen," is literally "fellow of the womb." The physical substance (consubstantiality) of siblings is from the mother, but their essential, eternal identity comes from the father. Although both men and women can be citizens, it remains the male's prerogative to transmit it (1995: 186).

Delaney's argument alerts us to the significance of the crossover between imageries of religion, kinship, gender, and nationality in making certain differences appear natural (cf. Yuval-Davis 1997; Bryant 2002).

For Schneider, it appeared that "Judaism is the clearest and simplest case where kinship, religion, and nationality are all a single domain" (1977: 70). While the most important criterion for being Jewish is birth, it is also the case that being a Jew relies not just on birth but on a specific and highly elaborated code of conduct. Schneider noted how the identity between religion, nation, and kinship posited in Judaism gave rise to particular problems for the modern nation-state of Israel. It is central to the ideology of nationhood in Israel that those who can claim to be Jewish by birth are also entitled to claim citizenship of the state of Israel (1977: 69). Susan Kahn's recent work on assisted conception in Israel (Kahn 2000) vividly illuminates the extraordinary lengths to which the state and the religious authorities in Israel go in order to reproduce citizenship. It is indicative of the pronatalist stance of the state that "in the mid-1990s, there were more fertility clinics per capita than in any other country in the world (twenty-four units for a population of 5.5 million, four times the number per capita in the United States)" (Kahn 2000: 2).

In Israel, family law is grounded in and informed by Jewish law. Analyzing cases where frozen sperm, originating from non-Jewish men in the United States, is used in the artificial insemination of ultra-Orthodox, infertile couples, and cases where ova are transferred from non-Jewish to Jewish women, Kahn documents the erasures accomplished by complex rabbinical debates and rulings in which genetic substance originating from non-Jews is "factored out" of the equation of what makes a Jew or a citizen of Israel. The debate over sperm procurement raises a number of problems for Orthodox Jews (Kahn 2000: 94–7). Among these is the question of whether, if the sperm was obtained from a Jewish source, the resultant child would be considered to have been born from an adulterous relationship (and hence be considered a *mamzer*, that is, the product of an illicit union, and therefore, together with his or her descendants for ten generations, not marriageable except to another *mamzer*). This problem is apparently obviated by the prescription to use non-Jewish sperm (2000: 104–10). Since Jewish status is transferred matrilineally, a child conceived by artificial insemination using non-Jewish sperm is still fully Jewish. The use of non-Jewish sperm also resolves the issue of the prohibition on masturbation for Jews, which is not binding for non-Jews. The completeness of the erasure is indicated by the fact that children born to different mothers from the same source of sperm are considered to be quite unrelated and may marry (2000: 104–5).

Matrilineal succession renders the problems raised by ova transmission even more complex and subject to intricate disagreements by rabbis on how to define motherhood (2000: 128–39). Kahn's extraordinary evocation of the Orthodox rabbinate's labyrinthine adjudications in Israel vividly illuminates Schneider's point. Here decisions about fertility and conception arrived at by rabbis define what constitutes a Jew and a citizen, and determine the reproduction of the nation-state of Israel (2000: 71–8).

Both the Turkish and the Israeli cases involve explicit discourses of naturalization in the ideology of nationhood. Such processes of naturalization have been the focus of recent analyses of nationalism and of conflict conceived in "ethnonationalist terms" (see Bryant 2002). But I suggest that the naturalization at work here is of a rather special kind. The deployment of an imagery of kinship in ideologies of nationalism is apparently so conventional as to be hardly worthy of comment. It recalls H. W. Fowler's distinction between "live" and "dead" metaphors – between metaphors that are used with a conscious aware-ness of the substitution, and those whose use is so conventional that the metaphor has become almost indistinguishable from the literal referent. But Fowler's warning is apt:

... the line of distinction between the live and the dead is a shifting one, the dead being sometimes liable, under the stimulus of an affinity or a repulsion, to galvanic stirrings, indistinguishable from life (Fowler 1965: 359).

Such "galvanic stirrings" have been evident in the all too frequent mo-ments in twentieth century history when the "diffuse, enduring solidar-ity" of the nation has been violently shattered. When warfare threatens, then calls to the fatherland or motherland in the name of the unity of the nation, or the solidarity of a brotherhood of fellow citizens, have a particular appeal.

But the violence of civil warfare, such as that seen in Bosnia and in Kosovo in the 1990s or in India at the time of the Partition, suggests that in certain negative circumstances the metaphors of kinship have the ability to take on meanings that are more literal than metaphorical. In such drastic moments of upheaval, commentators find themselves at a loss to account for the processes of destruction they witness. How is it possible for a war between "external" forces to become one that transforms longstanding neighbors into enemies? How can we account for the way in which, to cite Tone Bringa, documenting the Bosnian village where she worked:

Starting out as a war waged by outsiders, it developed into one where neigh-bour was pitted against neighbour after the familiar person next door had been made into a depersonalized alien, a member of the enemy ranks (Bringa 1995: xvi).

In the former Yugoslavia, as in India at the time of the Partition, the warfare that occurred was of an intimate kind. One of the means by which it was waged was through the sexual violation of women who were perceived as ethnically and religiously other. Veena Das (1995a) documents how in India pregnancies and children who resulted from abductions and violations of women posed rather different problems for the women most directly concerned, for their families, and for the state.

The families of origin of these women brought various strategies into play that rendered such women less visible, including marrying them off to close family, omitting them from family narratives, and crucially, very rarely claiming the children who resulted from such violations. The state, however, in adopting the responsibility for returning the women to their families of origin, not only invoked a language of national honor, but also made kinship norms considerably less flexible:

The interest in women . . . was premised upon their definition not as citizens but as sexual and reproductive beings. The honour of the nation was at stake because women as sexual and reproductive beings were forcibly held by the other side (Das 1995a: 221).

It is notable that in making it a matter of national honor to return these women to their families of origin, the state showed very little concern for the wishes of the women themselves. In many cases, it appears that the women had subsequently married, converted, and been absorbed into new families, and feared that they would be rejected by their families of origin. The state ignored such circumstances, forcing women to leave behind any children born to such unions when the women's families of origin refused to claim them. Das shows how in taking on these responsibilities, the state rendered women's definition as either Hindu or Muslim much less flexible. In constructing a singular category of "abducted women," which covered the multiple circumstances in which such unions had come about,[6] the state discourse made these women

---

[6] Das describes how during the Partition, interdenominational marriages sometimes occurred within a village specifically to prevent abduction by strangers. Legally, however, such marriages were not recognized, and the resulting children were considered illegitimate. The women were redefined as "abducted women" (1995a: 226).

more rather than less visible. Where local kinship norms allowed for absorption, the state discourse emphasized "purification" (1995a: 229).

In a separate essay on "The Anthropology of Pain," Das (1995b) reflects on the relation between bodily pain and its articulation in language and memory – both public and private. Noting how those who "betrayed" the ideologies of purity and honor by abandoning their kin at the time of the Partition were later obliterated from family narratives and from memory, she sees the rape and torture of women as a means of controlling the future. The infliction of pain on the bodies of victims is a means of actually making memories. And bodily experiences are not just an idiom for the *representation* of pain and trauma, or a kind of commentary upon it, but are part of that trauma (1995b: 186–8).

Such events contradict the conventional wisdom that the occurrence of a language of kinship in political discourses of nationalism is straightfor-wardly metaphorical. The threat and the reality of illicit kinship, brought about by violent means, are powerful factors in the disruption of in-tercommunal harmony. They are also, of course, frequently deployed in racist discourses. And this suggests that we should not take the apparent obviousness of the metaphor of the nation as family at face value. George Lakoff and Mark Johnson argue that "metaphors we live by" structure our actions and our experiences. The wide occurrence of phrases denot-ing a metaphorical concept such as "argument is war" reflects the way such metaphors structure "what we do and how we understand what we are doing when we argue" (Lakoff and Johnson 1980: 5). Such metaphors, they suggest, are so deeply embedded in culture that we may not see them as metaphors at all (1980: 66).

But does the image of nation as family operate in such a way? In part, it appears this image is utterly unremarkable, almost unconsciously evoked in the manner of Fowler's "dead metaphors." And, following Lakoff and Johnson's argument about the power of metaphor to structure our actions and experience, this image may go some way to explain the emotional appeal and the extraordinary sacrifices that nationalist ideologies evoke.

In part, however, the deployment of the language of kinship in political rhetoric is quite strategic and glaringly obvious. The heightened imagery may perhaps mislead us into thinking that the kinship of the nation is "mere" metaphor, a superficial phenomenon. But if we combine Lakoff and Johnson's insights with the observation that, in the extreme, this particular metaphor may transform itself into a quite literal reality, then perhaps we may begin to find an answer to Anderson's question about the emotional appeal of nationalism.

Conclusion

I began this chapter by describing two seemingly mundane and intimate contexts in which relationships can be transformed from a nonkinship basis into ones that operate in an idiom of kinship. In both Malaysia and Ecuador, such transformations invoke the symbolism of feeding. But these are not purely "domestic" processes. They have a political and economic import. In the Malay case, I have argued that the ease with which it was possible to transform strangers into kin was associated with a pattern of demographic mobility and the settlement of pioneer areas – in other words, with a regional politico-economy.

The ascription of fluidity and malleability to non-Western kinship occupies a familiar place in anthropological writings. But in my depiction of Western examples, I have attempted to demonstrate that kinship is equally open to manipulations and transformations. The active creation of kinship among gays in San Francisco, by adopted people in Scotland, or in ethnically plural Southall are nevertheless processes that, while drawing on an imagery of the domestic, have a wider significance. In urging a more thorough consideration of how substance and code can be combined or separated, and of what analytical labels like "fictive" kinship or "metaphorical" kinship imply, I suggest we may focus our attention on the active processes by which certain kinds of relationships are endowed with emotional power. And this is at the heart of what we must understand if Anderson's question about nationalism is to be answered – a need that seems even more pressing in the context of the ethnic strife that has dominated the political agenda in the Balkans, South Asia, the Middle East, and many parts of Africa at the close of the twentieth century and beginning of the twenty-first.

The combinations, separations, and recombinations of substance and code to which I have alluded in this chapter lie behind what Schneider termed the "blurred boundaries" between kinship, religion, and nationality. Here, I have highlighted the potential ideological and political salience of such moves. The slippage between what is metaphorical and what is literal makes the processes of naturalization at work in these separations and combinations of substance and code particularly difficult to grasp. I have suggested that the power of the hackneyed metaphor of the nation as family rests partly with its very familiarity. As a "metaphor we live by," it structures our experience of nationhood. But under extreme conditions, this metaphor can become a living actuality. And this slippage is a vital component of the force of kinship in the political realm. When the sexual violation of women threatens to result in the birth of children whose identities may be uncertain, problematic, or alien, then the call on national or communal loyalties comes to equate quite literally with loyalty to close kin. And here the emotional power of kinship becomes quite "unfamiliar." It can apparently call forth acts that turn "the familiar person next door" into "a depersonalized alien." It is because such processes must concern us as social scientists, and as citizens, that we should understand the mechanisms of kinship on which they rely.

SEVEN

Assisted Reproduction

In the previous chapter, a consideration of the ways in which relations that apparently have no basis in kinship may be cast in an idiom of kinship, or transformed over time into kin relations, led me to touch on processes of naturalization. The political salience of discourses about the nation that invoke naturalized images of the family would be hard to exaggerate. In this chapter, however, I look at naturalization from a different angle – that provided by recent advances in technologies of assisted reproduction.

Developments in reproductive medicine – including sperm and egg donation, surrogacy, in vitro fertilization, and cloning – have assumed a common currency in popular renditions of science and the family. The "technologization" of nature apparently has the potential to shake our most fundamental assumptions about kinship as a domain in which relations are given rather than produced through technological intervention. And this too gives rise to concerns that are publicly articulated and politically contested. It is not difficult to understand why recent studies in the sociology of science, as well as the anthropology of kinship, should have given so much attention to reproductive technologies. In this chapter, I take up some of this recent work and consider the significance of techno-logical advances in reproductive medicine both for academic knowledge practices and for everyday notions of kinship.

In tracing some of the debates about the different ways in which this technology affects practices and discourses of kinship, I want to resist not just an essentialization of kinship (which follows from my arguments in previous chapters) but also an essentialization of technology.[1] The manner in which different elements and qualities of technology are selected, highlighted, erased, or interwoven with aspects of kinship suggests quite complex, unpredictable, and creative processes at work when both experts and lay persons confront new developments in reproductive medicine.

From Sexual Procreation to Scientific Knowledge

David Schneider's *Critique of the Study of Kinship* (1984) was instrumental in highlighting the centrality of sexual procreation to anthropological definitions of kinship, just as his earlier analysis of *American Kinship* (1980) had demonstrated its centrality to indigenous American notions of kinship. The two projects were of course linked. Schneider had argued that "All of the significant symbols of American kinship are contained within the figure of sexual intercourse, itself a symbol of course" (1980: 40). In American culture, the family was conceived as "a 'natural' unit . . . based on the facts of nature" (1980: 33). In his later work, he showed how these assumptions of European and American culture had been incorporated into the anthropological analysis of kinship, which likewise assumed that sexual procreation was universally perceived as the basis of kinship. Using his own data on the Yapese, Schneider argued that such an assumption was not necessarily valid; certain cultures, including that of the Yapese, apparently did not link sexual intercourse and procreation. For Schneider, as I discussed in this book's introduction, this simply invalidated the basis on which the comparative study of kinship had been carried out. But the debate over the significance of apparently exotic beliefs about where babies come from was hardly a new one. Bronislaw Malinowski's (1929) depiction of Trobriand procreation

---

[1] I am indebted to Steve Gudeman for encouraging me to pursue this point here and elsewhere in this chapter.

beliefs had assured the topic's centrality for the decades that followed (see Leach 1967; Spiro 1968; Delaney 1986; Franklin 1997). And this close attention to the symbolic significance of sexual procreation in different cultures provides a line of continuity in anthropology that we can trace to recent studies focusing on the cultural implications of reproductive medicine in the West.

It is worth pausing for a moment to consider the relationship between nature and knowledge in Schneider's analysis of American culture, because this is an issue at the heart of more recent discussions of reproductive technology. The degree to which Schneider adhered to a view in which "biological facts" were cultural symbols rather than having a prior existence that culture then elaborated upon is somewhat unclear (see Carsten 1995a, 2000a; Franklin 1997: 54–5; Franklin 2001; Franklin and McKinnon 2001a). In spite of these tensions in the analytic status of "biology" in both *American Kinship* and *A Critique of the Study of Kinship*, Schneider had a key perception about the relation between scientific knowledge and kinship:

In American cultural conception, kinship is defined as biogenetic. This definition says that kinship is whatever the biogenetic relationship is. If science discovers new facts about biogenetic relationship, then that is what kinship is and was all along, although it may not have been known at the time (Schneider 1980: 23).

The idea that kinship in American culture is a direct reflection of current scientific knowledge about biogenetic connections passed with relatively little comment in *American Kinship*. However, given the pace of developments in the field of reproductive technology, the connection between scientific knowledge and kinship has become a key issue in the analysis of the social effects of this technology. Schneider himself commented nearly thirty years after the publication of *American Kinship*:

Nor did I notice until almost after it was done how much the Euro-American notion of knowledge depended on the proposition that knowledge is *discovered*, not invented, and that knowledge comes when the "facts" of nature which are hidden from us mostly, are finally revealed. Thus, for example, kinship was thought to be the social recognition of the actual facts of biological relatedness (Schneider 1995: 222; original italics).

That knowledge practices of the West hinge on an idea of a realm of nature "out there" to be discovered by science is an image made newly prominent – and problematic – not just by scientific advance itself, but also by the work of historians of science. Donna Haraway (1989, 1991, 1997), Bruno Latour (1993), Latour and S. Woolgar (1986), and others have shown the myriad ways in which "scientific facts," far from constituting a domain of pure truth, isolated from social context, and merely awaiting discovery, are actually shaped by laboratory practices, the milieux in which scientists work, their particular careers and gendered identities, and wider historical and cultural contexts.

The problematization of scientific truth as a late twentieth century phenomenon, which is highlighted in the work I have cited, is apparently itself an effect of an accelerated process of scientific advance and a simultaneous process of deconstruction that has marked the disciplines of the social sciences. Marilyn Strathern's work (1992a, 1992b) takes up the ways in which the extension of consumer choice to domains that paradigmatically were given rather than chosen has led to a destabilization of nature in late twentieth century English culture in the context of technological developments and a political ideology associated with Thatcherism. It is significant that she takes kinship as her example "that epitomises tradition under the pressure of change" (1992a: 10–11):

Kinship – or what English people refer to as family or relatives – is conventionally taken as embodying primordial ties that somehow exist outside or beyond the technological and political machinations of the world, that suffer change rather than act as a force for change. Indeed, the enduring ties of kinship may be regarded as archetypically traditional in antithesis to the conditions of modern life (1992a: 11).

But this tradition encapsulated in kinship is in fact intrinsic to the culture, which is modeled "after nature." As Strathern puts it, "Ideas about what is natural, primordial and embedded in the verities of family life are thereby made relevant to the present, will be refashioned for the future." (1992a: 11). In the English view, kinship is defined as the meeting place of culture and nature – simultaneously part of each – being both based in a nature that is itself regarded as the grounding for culture and also providing an image of the relation between cuture and nature (1992a: 198).

Strathern argues that in late twentieth century English culture, nature – which previously "had the status of a prior fact, a condition for existence" (1992a: 194) – has lost its "grounding function" as a condition for knowledge. This does not mean that nature has disappeared; to the contrary, it has become more evident. We are continually made aware of the nature that is under threat of being lost. But nature no longer constitutes the grounds for knowledge. What is taken to be natural has itself become a matter of choice. Whereas kin relationships previously would have been seen to have their basis in nature, and could be socially recognized or not, the effects of assisted reproduction are that relations can be perceived either as socially constructed or as natural relations assisted by technology. The more nature requires technological assistance, and the more social parenthood demands legislation, "the harder it is to think of a domain of natural facts independent of social intervention" (1992b: 30). If both kinship and knowledge had previously been seen as "a direct reflection of nature," as Schneider had observed, then it followed that these developments had destabilized not just kinship or nature, but knowledge itself.

The New, the Old, and the Not-So-Old

The discussions of the effects of reproductive technologies to which I have referred may seem rather abstract and academic. It is not immediately clear what implications, if any, these developments might have for everyday concepts and practices of relatedness. Strathern suggests that the scenario she outlines will certainly affect "the way people think about one another" (1992b: 30), but in what ways might this be happening? Do ordinary people pick and choose what to consider as "natural" in the manner she suggests? Is there a new arena of contestation about what nature is? Recent political confrontations in Britain, Europe, and North America over environmental concerns such as genetically modified (GM) crops, cloning, or animal husbandry do indeed suggest that nature has become a highly politicized and contested arena. But what of the impact on ideas and practices of relatedness?

One tension in the existing literature on the social effects of technological advances is between the depictions to which I have referred, which suggest a very radical shift in knowledge practices and in the way we think about kinship in the West, and those depictions that suggest that medical advances have really left most things unchanged or merely illuminate old certainties in new ways. I referred in Chapter 4 to Ray Abrahams's (1990) discussion of organ donation, aptly entitled "Plus ça Change, Plus C'est la Meme Chose?" Here organ donation is shown to reveal concerns that Abrahams suggests that anthropologists knew were there all along – over incest, for example, or a desire to limit kin ties (see also Edwards 1993, 2000).

Fenella Cannell (1990) discusses the debate surrounding two issues that were prominently featured in the English media in the mid-1980s. One was Victoria Gillick's campaign to prevent doctors from prescribing contraceptives to girls under sixteen without their parents' consent; the other was the discussion surrounding the Warnock Report – the published recommendations of the parliamentary Committee of Inquiry into Human Fertilisation and Embryology (Warnock Committee 1984). Cannell analyzes the way in which both debates reasserted "traditional" family values by raising two nightmare scenarios – in the former case, an image of underage girls able to have sex promiscuously without the possibility of reproduction; in the latter, of technology enabling reproduction without sex. Cannell demonstrates how the moral panic engendered by these contrastive images, and a third one raised by Gillick's own somewhat alarming fecundity as "a self-styled 'Catholic mother of ten'" (1990: 673), had the same effect: the reaffirmation of a positive image of the normal family reproducing naturally in a controlled way.

But there is surely more at issue here than the reassertion of what we knew all along. Sarah Franklin (1993) suggests that putting anthropological discussion of new technological developments in these terms simultaneously does two things. First, it foregrounds the symbolic importance of kinship by placing public debates over reproductive technology in a wider context of concerns about kinship. This may have the effect of putting the moral panic in perspective by showing how "'we' (the British) are engaged in something familiar, universal, and even traditional: the negotiation of the social and natural facts of kinship" (1993: 101). At the same time, anthropology's capacity to analyze these developments is also confirmed: "'We' (the anthropologists) have a discursive technology to describe what is occurring – it is called 'kinship'" (1993: 101). This reaffirmation of anthropological expertise in the area long held to be central to the discipline is worth pausing over. What is most striking, after all, is that it came precisely at a time when, as I argued in this book's introduction, kinship's place seemed to many to have become quite marginal within anthropology. To suggest that anthropology had the key to understanding the cultural effects of such recent developments was not simply to state an obvious truth, or even to stake a claim for anthropology vis-à-vis other disciplines, but to make a claim for kinship *within* anthropology.

Looking at recent anthropological publications on kinship, there can be little doubt that studies of assisted reproduction have been a source for the revitalization of kinship in anthropology (see, for example, Edwards 2000; Edwards et al. 1993; Franklin 1997; Franklin and Ragoné 1998; Ginsburg and Rapp 1991, 1995; Ragoné 1994; Rapp 1999; Strathern 1992a, 1992b). And the prevalence of such published studies may undermine the assertion that we are merely looking at something we knew all along. We need to be careful not to assume that when lay concerns about new technologies are phrased in terms of familiar anxieties about kin relationships – such as those surrounding incest, adultery, divorce and adoption – this means that we already know the cultural consequences of such developments. It would be indeed surprising if it were not the case that:

When people draw on what they already know to order and make sense of the ramifications of NRT [new reproductive technology], they frequently turn to analogies with the kinds of problems that arise in complex family relationships, such as those formed through divorce and adoption (Edwards 1993: 48).

But the concerns that Jeannette Edwards elucidates in discussions with people in Alltown, Lancashire, are not those that emerge from medical practioners or in parliamentary debates. Specifically, they highlight anxiety about the effects of technologies on *social* relationships, and they are phrased in terms of the existing relationships with which lay people are familiar and that cause concern (1993: 63; 2000: 223–7, 228–48).

Such concern about the consequences of technological intervention for social relationships emerges too in Helena Ragoné's (1994) study of surrogate mother programs in America. Ragoné shows how surrogate mothers are anxious to negate an image of themselves as motivated primarily by commercial concerns. By invoking an idiom of the gift, surrogate mothers substitute altruism and generosity for the financial gain that is deemed inimical to the realm of kinship (1994: 41, 59–60, 85). Significantly, this substitution simultaneously bypasses the relation between genetic father and surrogate mother, which carries connotations of adultery and illegitimacy, and focuses instead on sharing, reciprocity, and even sisterhood between the two women (1994: 124, 128).

Whether they are voiced by those directly involved in fertility treatment or by members of the general population, such concerns and the ways in which they are dealt with undoubtedly reveal quite familiar themes from the anthropological study of kinship. As Edwards observes, it would be surprising if this were not the case. But this does not foreclose the possibility of other, less recognizable, issues emerging in the contexts of assisted reproduction. Franklin's (1993) discussion of the debate in the British parliament on the Human Fertilisation and Embryology Act, which was passed in November 1990, provides a case in point. Franklin shows how, in the context of the parliamentary discussions, a rather "unfamiliar kinship" emerged. Central to the debate was the status of the human embryo. Franklin describes how both those in favor of allowing research on human embryos and those against such research held in common a view of "embyonic personhood" as uniquely individual and as biogenetically based. What divided proponents of research from those against it was the exact point at which such personhood was thought to arise. For opponents of research, individual personhood was believed to arise at the moment of fertilization, because of the presence of the individual's "unique genetic blueprint" made up of the combined genetic material of the egg and the sperm. Those in favor of research held that until the emergent spinal column (the "primitive streak") was formed, which is visible at about fourteen days, the embryo did not consitute a distinct individual (Franklin 1993: 102). Thus:

In agreement about the ingredients of personhood – an identifiable "starting point" defined as the emergence of a distinct individual biogenetic potential for development – the two sides disagreed over the exact point at which this occurred (Franklin 1993: 102).

While this concept of the biogenetic basis of personhood confirms a Schneiderian view of the basis of kinship in Euro-American cultures, Franklin also notes that, in accepting the "primitive streak" argument and imposing a legal limit of fourteen days during which research may be carried out, parliament substituted a "social" decision about time limits for a "natural" fact to which this natural fact was assumed to approximate.

Franklin's discussion highlights the ways in which the kinship discussed by members of the British parliament differed sharply from anything anthropologists would readily recognize as kinship. In particular, the focus on the embryo itself as an individualized, "prerelational" entity, divorced from its social context (revealed especially in the scarcity of references to its mother), suggests that embryos came to constitute a new type of kinship entity. In these debates, the embryo emerged as an emblem of a shared humanity embodying not specific kin ties, but a biological development that all human beings hold in common (1993: 106–10). Where kinship was the subject of discussion, it was in the form of kinship *potential* – once again represented by the embryo. Here the embryo embodied a kind of "kinship yet-to-be," made possible by science and technology rather than nature (1993: 126). This is a crucial shift. In rendering the mother invisible, the kinship embodied by the nonrelational embryo is, as Franklin puts it, "technologised and geneticised, . . . [and] also highly individualised" (1993: 128). This kinship, which is grounded in technological assistance rather than in nature, begins to look rather less familiar to anthropologists. Far from embodying natural certainties, it encapsulates the uncertain consequences of scientific advance. And it is the perceived threat of the unknowable results of scientific progress that Franklin suggests is evident in the heightened emotional register in which the legislation was discussed.

Naturalizing Technology; Technologizing Nature

So far, the studies of assisted reproduction to which I have referred might be adduced as depicting some familiar kinship concerns found among "ordinary" – that is, nonexpert – people, in contrast to the less familiar kinship issues raised in legislative, scientific, or medical contexts. The British parliamentary discussions are of interest, partly because in some sense they appear to bring a rather rarified and legalistic discussion "home" to those who might consider themselves expert in matters of kinship but nonexpert in the field of medical technology (everyone, as Franklin notes, including members of parliament, has relations). If these debates make evident new kinds of kinship, then this may be taken to suggest that Strathern's predictions about the effects of reproductive technologies are not restricted to an abstract academic context.

On the other hand, the juxtaposition of legal or medical contexts with more everyday circumstances in which lay people talk about their concerns in terms of incest, adultery, or illegitimacy recalls a contrast I mapped out in an earlier discussion of personhood in Chapter 4. We saw there how a concern for the bounded individual was particularly prominent in Western legal, religious, and philosophical debates about the person. But in other contexts, particularly those concerning kinship, a relational view of the person was much more evident. This raises the question of how nonexpert views about kinship are modified in direct encounters with fertility treatments and with medical staff.

Franklin's (1997) study of women's experience of IVF (in vitro fertilization) in two infertility clinics in Britain recounts how the literature provided to patients describes the technology as giving nature a "helping hand" – in this sense, it is "just like nature" (209–10). The patients themselves also express this view:

You hear all these things about test-tube babies and I think a lot of people think that it's quite an abnormal process, and I don't think we really appreciated what's involved. And I think we thought it was all a bit, um, clinical and – I mean I don't think we realised what a natural process it was, I mean it's only sort of emulating a natural process . . . (Kate Quigley, cited in Franklin 1997: 187).

Simultaneously, reproductive biology is denaturalized – it can be assisted by technology. Indeed, Franklin documents how IVF is said both to emulate natural processes and at the same time comes to be seen as something special or "miraculous." But this miracle then comes to define natural conception too. As one patient puts it, "I mean it's a miracle anyway when anybody has a child, but it just seems to be an even bigger miracle I'm trying to achieve . . . " (cited in Franklin 1997: 188). That natural conception can ever be successful without technological assistance is itself construed as miraculous. Reproduction thus becomes a technological achievement rather than a natural sequence of events (Franklin 1998: 103). Kinship is no longer given, defined against "natural," "biological" facts; nature and technology have become mutually substitutable (1997: 210–13).

The substitutions of course imply that, in some contexts at least, the line between what is attributed to technology and what to nature may become quite blurred. And this may not be seen in benign terms. As technology apparently comes to occupy an ever larger space, intervening between the realms of nature and culture, these two domains, as well as the boundary between them, are increasingly subject to contestation. The highly politicized debates to which I briefly alluded earlier in this chapter over GM crops, cloning, or the Human Genome Project are just some of the many manifestations of the ways in which both nature and technology are contested areas. Public concern over the role of technology and the apparently increasing and self-propelling dominance of technology over many aspects of life – and particularly over reproductive processes – is expressed in myriad ways, from environmental activism to fictional accounts. Images of technology "out of control" suggest a perception that technology itself – although produced by humans – has become an objectified force unmoored from human control.

But how does the substitution between nature and culture, or the increasing space occupied by technology in reproduction, affect the kin relations involved? Here I think the studies we have are less conclusive – partly because they tend to focus on couples undergoing treatment, and on the complex negotiation of medical processes in which they participate, rather than on what happens to kin relations outside these contexts or once treatment is over. In these rather narrow confines, we can discern the twin effects of a technologization of nature and a naturalization of technology. But it is difficult to know how these negotiations are incorporated into existing kin relations or how they will affect future ones.

Edwards's (2000) illuminating study of kinship idioms in urban Lancashire, to which I have already referred, is unusual in documenting the concerns about reproductive technologies expressed by those who have no direct experience of them. Edwards demonstrates how idioms of kinship, rather than constituting a clearly bounded domain, emerge from a diverse field of concerns and discourses about, for example, local history, landscape, naming, class, and so on. Conversely, the way people view reproductive technologies interweaves with, and feeds back into, these various overlapping fields. Edwards's work is suggestive of the complex manner in which different elements are brought into play or ignored in people's kinship practices and discourses.

Another example, this time taken from Janelle Taylor's (1998) Chicago-based study of the social effects of using ultrasound techniques to monitor women's pregnancies, suggests that use of the technology fundamentally affects a woman's relationship to the fetus inside her. Once again, however, the shifts involved appear quite contradictory. Here the contradiction is inherent in the two processes of "psychological benefit" that ultrasound is supposed to foster – one is bonding between mother and child, and the other is offering reassurance to the mother. Of course, reassurance is achieved only if the results of the tests do not reveal fetal abnormalities – and detection of abnormalities is the medical justification for the procedure in the first place. As Taylor observes, ultrasound procedures involve a depiction of pregnancy as a conditional and fragile state "subject to pre-natal testing and quality control," but these same tests are supposed to promote unconditional and absolute bonding between mother and child. Here maternal–infant bonding theory has been extended to focus not just on the period after birth but during pregnancy. And once again, "natural" mother love can be achieved only through the intervention of technology. The visual nature of the technology itself, however, makes the mother a "spectator" in the "entertainment" of viewing her own pregnancy through ultrasound techniques – and it is clear that medical staff are not at ease with this aspect of women's consumption of screening (1998: 29–32).

Taylor suggests that in these moves, while the fetus is constructed as a "consumer product," its personhood simultaneously is established early in its prenatal existence. But it is difficult to anticipate the likely longer-term effects on relations between mother and child, father and child, or between parents for the majority of those who undergo ultrasound monitoring.[2]

Recognizing Relations

One study that offers highly suggestive insights as to how technological intervention may affect the categorization of kin relations is Charis Cussins Thompson's work (Cussins 1997, 1998; Thompson 2001) in American infertility clinics. Thompson (2001) explicitly sets out to reveal the strategies by which patients delineate who the mother is in cases where technological intervention results in more than one possible candidate for this role. Although her study is restricted to the clinical context, Thompson notes that not only does research conducted in the clinic allow us to see the articulation of the public and the private, but it also "illustrates flexibility in biological and scientific practice" (2001: 190).

In the cases of gestational surrogacy and in vitro fertilization with ovum donation, which Thompson analyzes, a range of strategies is deployed for delineating the mother and excluding other possible candidates for the role. Those involved draw not only on biology and nature, but on various socioeconomic factors, including who is paying for treatment, who

---

[2] See Rayna Rapp's (1999) extraordinarily rich and detailed study of amniocentesis for an analysis of the social affects of prenatal genetic testing, particularly for Down's syndrome. This work successfully confronts many of the methodological difficulties and constraints of studying reproductive technologies in their diverse social contexts. What emerges is a very complex set of scenarios in which scientific knowledge and a discourse of risk are filtered through the differentiated experiences, histories, and class backgrounds of those involved.

owns the gametes and embryos, who is providing the sperm, and who will have future parenting responsibility for the child. What is particularly interesting about this material is the way in which the protagonists skillfully transform biological kinship by mapping genetics back onto socioeconomic factors. Thus in one case Thompson cites, Paula, an African American woman, describes how important it is to choose an egg donor from her "community." She justifies this view in terms of being merely a continuation of historical practice: "something we've been doing all along" (2001: 182). Paula refers here to African American women acting as "mother" or "second mother" to close female relative's or friend's children. Here donor egg IVF is described in terms of already existing practices. Paula focuses on the sharing of ethnicity with the egg donor rather then separating her own genetic identity, or "natural kinship," from that of the donor. Thus the child's "community" is prioritized over the individual genetic identity of the mother.

In another case, Giovanna, an Italian American woman, has chosen a friend who is also Italian American as egg donor. Giovanna alludes both to emotional closeness with her friend, and to a "genetic similarity" arising from shared ethnicity, in explaining her choice. But she also casts her own gestational role in biological terms rather than in social ones: "the baby would grow inside her, nourished by her blood and made out of the very stuff of her body all the way from a four-celled embryo to a fully formed baby" (Thompson 2001: 180). In speaking in such terms, Thompson notes how Giovanna has separated the natural basis of motherhood into different components in terms of genetics and bodily substance. In a further move, the supposed "genetic similarity" between donor and recipient is talked about in terms of similar home influences and a shared culture. Here "the reduction to genes is only meaningful because it codes back to sociocultural aspects of being Italian American (it is not unidirectional)" (2001: 181). Ethnicity thus elides nature and culture, "collecting disparate elements and linking them without any assumption that every one of the sociocultural aspects of having an Italian American mother, for example, needs to map back onto biology" (2001: 181). It is this complex and so-phisticated interweaving, or flexible "choreography between the natural and the cultural" (2001: 198), that enables those undergoing treatment to arrive at their own appropriate destinations in terms of how relationships should be mapped out.

Thompson's work stands out for a number of reasons. First, she demonstrates just how underdetermined and variable are the connections between biological and social kinship, and how adeptly and flexibly they can be manipulated. Biology here is very far from providing a mono-lithic or simple basis for kinship. And Thompson's work begins to fill in the gaps left by Schneider's assertion that kinship in American culture is "whatever the biogenetic relationship is." Second, we can begin to see in detail some of the ways technology permits both new and old claims to identity. Far from simply providing a means to essentialize genetics, the technology offers various possibilities for transforming biology – by coding it back to socioeconomic or cultural factors. Indeed, what is par-ticularly suggestive about this work are the connections Thompson draws between the uptake of technological innovations and the patient's own explicit recognition and categorization of kin relations. Her evaluation of the prognosis of the cases she considers implies that the ways in which these protagonists will experience kinship in the future will eventually feed back into the experience of technology.

New Kinds of Relations? New Modes of Reckoning?

At various points in this book I have introduced material in which kinship in the West takes on apparently new guises. In Chapter 4, I discussed Diane Blood's attempts to create a child using her dead husband's frozen sperm. In Chapter 6, I referred to Susan Kahn's work on assisted reproduction in Israel, where some quite elaborate moves are played out in order to erase non-Jewish substance and to reproduce both individual persons and the nation-state of Israel. In the same chapter, we saw how adopted people see their search for birth kin as helping to define who they are in a way that is socially meaningful – even when the reunions themselves may not result in establishing viable relations with birth kin.

The kinship revealed in these stories defies any simplified reading. If we look at it again in the light of the analyses I have presented in this chapter, what is striking is that although one might expect in all these cases to see an essentialist and geneticist understanding of kinship coming to the fore (cf. Finkler 2000), the reality is much more complex. The birth parent reunion stories I gathered seemed to suggest a step toward some kind of genetic "foundations," but, the results showed a sophisticated and highly variable articulation of what is thought to originate in genetics and what is provided by the environment. Here consciously undertaken searches to delineate origins do not necessarily end up supporting a geneticist definition of kinship. And similarly, the highly visible moves deployed by the Orthodox rabbinate in Israel to define who is a Jew and a citizen of Israel in cases of assisted conception have in the end very little to do with genetics, although they apparently rely on sophisticated genetic arguments. Diane Blood's desire to produce an heir to her husband and to reproduce within her marriage, the adoptees' search for their origins, the rabbinate's attempts to define Jewish citizens – all bear some similarity to the manner in which the patients studied by Thompson go through a range of variable maneuvers to delineate who is the mother in cases of assisted conception.

All of these scenarios involve participants deploying genetic arguments in a highly visible manner. But the results of these articulations show no retreat to a simplified and geneticized reading of kinship. Instead, we have seen how those concerned are able to achieve a complex "choreography" between social and biological factors.

Here, however, we need to be careful to distinguish what is old and what is new. Returning for a moment to Strathern's discussion of what the old kinship took for granted may be helpful. Kinship, in its familiar English guise, apparently had about it a quiet politesse; choices could be made – for example, one could choose precisely which kin one failed to keep in touch with. But, for the most part, the etiquette of kinship prescribed that this ought to happen in a discreet, almost hidden, manner. Indeed, this is the classic terrain of family secrets. What Edwards and Strathern (2000) describe as the "interdigitation" of biological and social factors in the reckoning of kinship involves making inclusions and exclusions. Such exclusions occur not just through the accumulation of omissions, simply forgetting or failing to make contact and eventually losing touch with a kinsperson who has moved away or ceased to be important. Exclusions are moves that make kinship manageable in situations where there are potentially endless relations to whom one might be connected (Edwards and Strathern 2000). It is neither the availability of a geneticist repertoire nor the possibility of ceasing to recognize kin that is new here. As Strathern has commented, "there was always a choice as to whether or not biology is made the foundation of relationships" (Strathern 1993: 196; cited in Hayden 1995: 45).

What is most striking about the stories of "new kinship" to which I have referred is not so much the newness of the kinship that results, but the very explicitness of the moves by which people are able to define who is kin and who is not, and what kinds of kinship count and what kinds do not. In these definitional moves, a multiplicity of factors and characteristics can be brought to bear upon each other, and this multiplicity resists any essentializing analytic frame.

If explicitness and a more or less visible reshuffling of the elements of kinship are what strike us most readily about kinship's new forms, then it is worth asking why they should jar. What is startling here is the very obviousness of the moves to exclude or include. Kinship, grounded in nature, as Strathern has argued, was precisely considered taken for granted rather than a matter for choice. Exercising choice in such a highly visible and explicit manner thus has the force of destabilizing that taken-for-granted quality of the relations themselves.

This quality then is one aspect of what is apparently different about the "new kinship." But if it marks a cultural shift, this shift is not confined to domestic or private contexts. Intense media debates, publicly voiced concern, and legislative innovations over new forms of family, and the "rights" of parents to have children or even of children to divorce their parents (cf. Simpson 1998: 76) underline the political salience of contestations over the domain of the family and of the symbolic space that kinship will occupy in the future. And as I have suggested, these public debates can be linked to the larger contestations over increasing encroachments by technology on what previously was seen as the domain of the natural.

But before we are too quick to predict a realm of relations designated by choice, in which individuality is inscribed onto ever-smaller body parts or ever earlier manifestations of life and is essentialized in terms of genetically carried attributes, it is worth recalling some of the conflicting pieces of evidence we have available. For, although legal arguments about custody or ethics often appear to hinge on a view of persons as uniquely defined by their genetic make-up from long before birth (see Dolgin 1995, 1997), what is also clear from the material I have presented here is that we do not necessarily find evidence of a highly geneticized view of kinship where we might most expect to find it. And, by the same token, although embryos may constitute new individualized kinship entities endowed with the qualities of personhood in the womb or in the petri dish, there is also evidence of assisted reproduction leading to new kinds of relations conceived in terms very different from individuality.

Monica Konrad's (1998) London-based study of women who act as egg donors in fertility clinics suggests that, instead of seeing themselves as providing unique, autonomous, and individualized genetic material, these women perceive themselves as donating body parts that are without inherent biogenetic properties. One woman describes it in the following way: "I don't think the eggs are mine, they're not something physical that they're my eggs. I don't even think of them as eggs." Another says, "They're just like a fingernail or something ... they're just a normal part, like any other part" (cited in Konrad 1998: 651). This usage contrasts in every way with the heightened emotional tones of parliamentarians, cited by Franklin, discussing embryos. The gifts of eggs that women donate are given to help other women conceive, in generalized terms, rather than being thought of as already formed halves of new genetic identities. Donors see themselves as simply furnishing a means for "starting off" a process that the recipients will "finish" (1998: 652). Rather than talking in terms of body parts that are "owned," these women see themselves as being part of a joint effort to help infertile women conceive.

Konrad elucidates how the process of extracting eggs, which uses chemical products taken from numerous other women, as well as the multiple directions in which the eggs subsequently travel when several women may become recipients from a single donor, mean that the original source of eggs becomes obscure. This facilitates what she calls "a non-possessive modeling of these a-genetically 'shared,' anonymously pooled, body parts" (1998: 653). It is significant that donor women articulate their desire to help not in terms of reproducing particular identities, but in terms of generality and anonymity – a wish "to help busloads of women," as one informant put it (1998: 656). What is especially thought-provoking about Konrad's analysis is her attentiveness to the imaginary space that "the discursive substance of anonymity" (1998: 655) comes to occupy for her informants. Emphasizing the shared effort and substance involved in this kind of reproduction and creating value out of the very diffuseness and generality of the relations involved bring into play not the heavy obligations of kinship but enchantment, hope, and excitement (659–61).

I find this sense of excitement afforded by the "sociality of anonymity" infectious. It suggests that assisted reproduction does not just raise concerns with which we were already familiar – although Konrad nicely juxtaposes her material with Melanesian ethnography of personhood, relations, and body parts. Nor are we necessarily entering an era in which the identity of persons is constrained by an ever-increasing concern for bounded individuals with discrete and singly owned body parts, whose genetic endowment has determined who they are even before birth.

The imagination that ordinary people put to work when they participate in new forms of kinship – whether it be donating eggs, searching for birth kin, or ascribing motherhood – involves a subtle and sophisticated articulation of the many factors that may create kinship. That the results of this imaginative work are sometimes quite unpredicted and sometimes throw into relief concerns that seem more familiar may be faintly reassuring. Both the surprises and the familiarities offered by new forms of kinship in the West should encourage anthropologists not to retreat from the non-Western cultures that have been so central to the comparative study of kinship. For it is in defamiliarizing what seems most familiar about the new kinship and by illuminating the unexpected that the analytical inspiration provided by comparison will give new scope to the study of kinship.

EIGHT

Conclusion

I began this book with three vignettes: Diane Blood's attempt, conducted through the British courts, to use her deceased husband's sperm in fertility treatment; a Scottish woman's account of her search for her birth mother from whom she had been separated in infancy; and the debates of the Orthodox rabbinate over the procurement and use of non-Jewish sperm in Israel. What do these stories reveal, I asked, and what do they have in common? Above all, why do they matter?

In search of further inspiration, I have glanced through newspaper clippings from the turn of the new century on issues that are salient to public debate on family and kinship. I am struck both by the range of issues and by the prominence of their coverage. There are four that particularly catch my attention. The first is a report on the suffering of birth fathers whose babies had been put up for adoption ("I can still smell my baby's scent. It's always with me" [*The Guardian*, 9.8.00]). The second is the decision by the British government to allow cells to be taken from embryos less than fourteen days old for the purposes of research on degenerative diseases – the use of embryonic stem cells for therapeutic cloning ("Medical Science at New Frontier," *The Guardian*, 17.8.00). Third comes the announcement of new proposals that babies conceived after their father's death – who are currently legally fatherless – will have the right to have the name of their father on their birth certificate ("Birth Certificates to Carry Names of Fathers Who Die," *The Scotsman*, 26.8.00).

Diane Blood, whose baby Liam was born in 1998 but who was not allowed to put her dead husband's name on her son's birth certificate, is reported as commenting, "It is very important for these children and their mothers because it means that the biological facts will be recorded as they truly are" (*The Guardian*, 26.8.00). Finally, a report on new international research on children born as the result of fertility treatment using anonymously donated sperm apparently reveals that they are likely to suffer trauma and feelings of abandonment similar to that of adopted children when they discover the truth about their conception ("Children Born by Donated Sperm 'Liable to Suffer Identity Crisis,'" *The Guardian*, 31.8.00).

The stories it seems are endless. I could find four more for any month in the last year. They suggest that both the nature of ties between mothers or fathers and their children and the legal entailments that follow are subjects for a great deal of contemporary concern. So too are the issues of identity that these ties – or their severance – set in motion. What point constitutes the beginning of life, what are the ethical boundaries of research on human embryos, or the boundaries between one life and another – all these are subjects of debate and moral dilemma. But why should all this matter to anthropologists?

Instead of finding an answer, or perhaps because the answer is after all quite apparent, I have taken a long way round – traversing houses, gender, personhood, substance, idioms of kinship that are not traced to sexual procreation, and reproductive technologies. But it is time to return to the questions with which I began. The three stories with which I began this book, as well as those I have culled from the newspapers more recently, suggest a considerable and very explicit unease about what kinship is, and what it should mean, at the beginning of the twenty-first century. This unease translates itself into some quite remarkable debates and contestations in which the rights and obligations of kinship are apparently renegotiated.

I have tried to highlight how these rather unfamiliar forms of kinship are constructed out of both old and new materials. I am equally struck by

Monica Konrad's unexpected description, to which I referred at the end of Chapter 7, of the "sociality of anonymity" in the kinship imaginary of egg donors, and by the apparently anachronistic appearance of a ouija board that occurred in the highly contemporary narrative about a search for birth kin with which I opened the introduction. Perhaps these two are appropriate framing devices for the new kinship. The ouija board is evoked as a tool to re-create a kinship that is supposedly founded on "natural connection," while a connectedness built out of anonymity is envisaged in the context of kinship created in the highly technologized surroundings of the modern fertility clinic. But of course both the ouija board, as a conveyor of natural connection, and the sociality of anonymity, which is a tangental result of fertility treatment, are very much part of contemporary Western kinship. The recombinations and reimaginings of kinship are constructed out of both the old and the new.

What is startling here is not so much the reconfigurations that kinship undergoes – since it is a fiction that kinship ever constituted some kind of intransigent rock on which more malleable and dynamic forms of sociality were superimposed – but the obviousness of the maneuvers involved. To cite Diane Blood again, the literalism behind the idea that there is some kind of moral imperative for "the biological facts" to "be recorded as they truly are" is at first glance what seems most like kinship as it has always been. But actually, this is what is most different about contemporary Western kinship. What is so arresting is the very explictness with which one person's rights are weighed against another's, one kind of connection is compared to another, and one source of bodily substance is erased while another is highlighted. If, from an anthropological perspective, it is the transparency of moves of inclusion and exclusion that seems most unfamiliar about the new kinship, then this should perhaps alert us to the significance of what has always remained implicit, not just in everyday versions of kinship but also in anthropological understandings.

The arguments of this book have been arranged as a critical commentary on a set of dichotomies that have been as fundamental to the

anthropological study of kinship as they have to Western folk notions –
between nature and culture, between the biological and the social, and
more recently, between substance and code. These dichotomies have
informed anthropologists' definitions of what should constitute their
proper field of study, ever since Lewis Henry Morgan proposed the distinction between classificatory and descriptive systems of terminology.
David Schneider's work marked a crucial turning point, however, in
foregrounding the connection between analytical definitions of kinship
and Western folk notions. The effect of his work was simultaneously to
shut down the field of kinship as a subject for exciting new studies and to
put a whole new range of problems on the agenda. After Schneider, anthropologists could no longer simply put what is "biological" in kinship
to one side as something that did not concern them. It is no coincidence
that crosscultural studies of the symbolism and cultural meaning of procreation became the focus for a great deal of anthropological interest –
perhaps often to the puzzlement of the anthropologists' informants.

I have taken the culturalist critique of kinship as my starting point,
but part of my project has been to assess where that critique leads. It
sometimes seems as though, after Schneider, anthropologists were left
with no alternative but simply to document how, in such and such a
culture, procreation, marriage, or death was understood quite differently
(cf. Holy 1996). If that is where the culturalist turn leads, it is, I think, in
the end unsatisfactory. Because I find this strategy insufficient for analysis,
I have scrutinized Schneider's deployment of the dichotomous orders of
nature and law and of substance and code at some length.

In Chapter 5 I cited Schneider's bald assertion that in America, "kinship
is whatever the biogenetic relationship is. If science discovers new facts
about the biogenetic relationship, then that is what kinship is, and was
all along, although it may not have been known at the time" (Schneider
1980: 23). I hope that some of the complex trackings documented in this
book between "biogenetic relations" and "kinship" – whether they are
made by adopted people attempting to reinsert themselves into the lives

of their birth kin, by those undergoing fertility treatment, or by those engaging in rabbinical debates over the proper sources and uses of sperm under Jewish law – have shown the inadequacy of Schneider's statement as a description of kinship in the West. Diane Blood's comment on the importance of recording "biological facts. . . . as they truly are" on British birth certificates highlights how this tracking between biology and kinship is part of a two-way process. Sometimes scientific understandings of procreation may determine kinship relations, but often the recognition of kinship involves a far more complex interplay, or "flexible choreography" (Thompson 2001), between many different factors that are not necessarily themselves easily labeled as "social" or "biological." And this is partly because the boundaries of what is constituted by biology or kinship are not set in stone, but may shift or merge in relation to each other.

The problematization of the boundary between what is social and what is biological in kinship should not, however, be taken as a kind of antidualist stance for its own sake. I have nothing in particular against dichotomies. There is no doubt that an opposition between nature and culture has been at the heart of Euro-American ideas for several hundred years, and it may well constitute the local manifestation of a distinction that is perhaps universally made between what is "given" and what is "made" (cf Astuti 1998; Lambek 1998). But Schneider's work began to illuminate how that dichotomy had been implicitly incorporated into anthropological analyses of kinship. Because anthropological understandings of kinship presumed what they should have subjected to analytic scrutiny, the comparative project that is at the heart of anthropology was short-circuited.

In a similar context, I have referred to Bruno Latour's (1993) argument that the modernity of the West, which rests on a separation of the domains of nature and culture, is a myth (see Carsten 2000a). Latour argues that in fact "we have never been modern," in the sense that the domains of nature and culture are kept separate only by a constant effort of what he calls "purification," which is at the heart of how scientific discovery is construed. Nature, he argues, is actually constructed in the laboratory by scientists who are immersed in their particular social and political milieux. Latour extends an enticing invitation to engage in a "new comparative anthropology" that, by admitting that "culture is an artefact created by bracketing nature off" (1993: 104), abandons the divide between nature and society.

If it remains somewhat unclear how exactly we might go about the comparison of "nature–cultures" that Latour advocates, there is something here that is worth pausing over. What I find liberating in Latour's abandonment of "the Great Divide" is that if we apply it to the field of kinship, it at once reconfigures the analytical domain that kinship occupies. It does so in two ways: first, by not assuming a particular relation or boundary between nature and culture; and second, by putting the West into the same analytical frame as non-Western cultures. We can then no longer sustain the notion that whereas "they" have kinship, "we" have families, just as we cannot assume that, whereas in the West what is social and what is biological are firmly and clearly separated in opposed domains, in non-Western cultures they are inextricably mixed up. What is liberating in Latour's vision is that this might offer a route to a different kind of comparative project.

In fact, I would rephrase Latour's point about abandoning the nature–culture divide. Rather than moving away from this distinction, we need to make it the subject of proper scrutiny. It is precisely the ways in which people in different cultures distinguish between what is given and what is made, what might be called biological and what might be called social, and the points at which they make such distinctions, that, without preconceptions, should be at the center of the comparative anthropological analysis of kinship. If we can manage to place side by side the ouija board and the Malay house, the sociality of anonymity and the Ecuadorean meal, or Tallensi personhood and organ donation in the United Kingdom, then we might be on the way to achieving a new kind of comparative understanding of kinship.

Bibliography

Abrahams, Ray. 1990. "Plus ça Change, Pluc C'est la Même Chose?" *Australian Journal of Anthropology* 1: 131–46.

Anderson, Benedict. 1983. *Imagined Communities: Reflections on the Origin and Spread of Nationalism.* London: Verso.

——— 1990. "The Idea of Power in Javanese Culture," in *Language and Power: Exploring Political Cultures in Indonesia.* Ithaca, NY: Cornell University Press.

Appadurai, Arjun. 1988. "Is Homo Hierarchicus?" *American Ethnologist* 15: 745–61.

Astuti, Rita. 1993. "Food for Pregnancy: Procreation, Marriage and Images of Gender among the Vezo of Madagascar," *Social Anthropology* 1, 3:1–14.

——— 1995a. *People of the Sea: Identity and Descent among the Vezo of Madagascar.* Cambridge, UK: Cambridge University Press.

——— 1995b. "'The Vezo Are Not a Kind of People': Identity, Difference and 'Ethnicity' among a Fishing People of Western Madagascar," *American Ethnologist* 22, 3: 464–82.

——— 1998. "'It's a Boy, It's a girl!': Reflections on Sex and Gender in Madagascar and Beyond," in Andrew Strathern and Michael Lambek (eds.), *Bodies and Persons: Comparative Perspectives from Africa and Melanesia.* Cambridge, UK: Cambridge University Press.

Atkinson, Jane. 1990. "How Gender Makes a Difference in Wana Society," in Jane Atkinson and Shelly Errington (eds.), *Power and Difference: Gender in Island Southeast Asia.* Stanford, CA: Stanford University Press.

——— 1996. "Quizzing the Sphinx: Reflections on Mortality in Central Sulawesi," in Laurie J. Sears (ed.), *Fantasizing the Feminine in Indonesia.* Durham, NC: Duke University Press.

Bachofen, Johan. 1861. *Das Mutterrecht.* Basel: Schwabe.

Bahloul, Joelle. 1996. *The Architecture of Memory: A Jewish-Muslim Household in Colonial Algeria, 1937–1962.* Cambridge, UK: Cambridge University Press.

Bibliography

Banks, David J. 1976. "Islam and Inheritance in Malaya: Culture, Conflict or Islamic Revolution?" *American Ethnologist* 3 (4): 573–86.

Barnard, Alan and Anthony Good. 1984. *Research Practices in the Study of Kinship*. London: Academic Press.

Barnes, J. A. 1962. "African Models in the New Guinea Highlands." *Man* (n.s.) 62: 5–9.

Barnett, Steve. 1976. "Coconuts and Gold: Relational Identity in a South Indian Caste," *Contributions to Indian Sociology* (n.s.) 10: 133–56.

Baumann, Gerd. 1995. "Managing a Polyethnic Milieu: Kinship and Interaction in a London Suburb," *JRAI* (n.s.) 1: 725–41.

Bloch, Maurice. 1983. *Marxism and Anthropology*. Oxford, UK: Oxford University Press.

1988. "Death and the Concept of the Person," in S. Cederroth, C. Corlin, and J. Lundstrom (eds.), *On the Meaning of Death: Essays on Mortuary Rituals and Eschatological Beliefs* (Uppsala Studies in Cultural Anthropology, No. 8). Stockholm: Almqvist and Wicksell International.

1993. "Zafimaniry Birth and Kinship theory," *Social Anthropology* 1a: 119–32.

1995. "The Resurrection of the House among the Zafimaniry of Madagascar," in Janet Carsten and Stephen Hugh-Jones (eds.), *About the House: Lévi-Strauss and Beyond*. Cambridge, UK: Cambridge University Press.

Borneman, John. 1992. *Belonging in the Two Berlins: Kin, State, Nation*. Cambridge, UK: Cambridge University Press.

Bouquet, Mary. 1993. *Reclaiming English Kinship: Portuguese Refractions on English Kinship Theory*. Manchester, UK: Manchester University Press.

1996. "Family Trees and Their Affinities: The Visual Imperative of the Genealogical Diagram," *JRAI* (n.s.) 2: 43–66.

2000. "Figures of Relations: Reconnecting Kinship Studies and Museum Collections," in J. Carsten 2000 (ed.), *Cultures of Relatedness: New Approaches to the Study of Kinship*. Cambridge, UK: Cambridge University Press.

Bourdieu, Pierre. 1977. *Outline of a Theory of Practice*. Cambridge, UK: Cambridge University Press.

1990. *The Logic of Practice*. Translated by Richard Nice. Cambridge, UK: Polity Press.

Bowen, John R. 1993. *Muslims through Discourse*. Princeton, NJ: Princeton University Press.

Brenner, Sujanne A. 1995. "Why Women Rule the Roost: Rethinking Javanese Ideologies of Gender and Self-Control," in Aihwa Ong and Michael G. Petetz (eds.), *Bewitching Women, Pious Men: Gender and Body Politics in Southeast Asia*. Berkeley and Los Angeles, CA: University of California Press.

Bibliography

Bringa, Tone. 1995. *Being a Muslim the Bosnian Way: Identity and Community in a Central Bosnian Village*. Princeton, NJ: Princeton University Press.

Bryant, Rebecca. 2002. "The Purity of Spirit and the Power of Blood: A Comparative Perspective on Nation, Gender and Kinship in Cyprus," *Journal of the Royal Anthropological Institute (JRAI)* (n.s.) 8 (3): 509–30.

Busby, Cecilia. 1997a. "Of Marriage and Marriageability: Gender and Dravidian Kinship," *JRAI* (n.s.) 3: 21–42.

1997b. "Permeable and Partible Persons: A Comparative Analysis of Gender and Body in South India and Melanesia," *JRAI* (n.s.) 3: 261–78.

2000. *The Performance of Gender: An Anthropology of Everyday Life in a South Indian Fishing Village*. London, UK, and New Brunswick, NJ: Athlone Press.

Butler, Judith. 1990. *Gender Trouble: Feminism and the Subversion of Identity*. New York and London: Routledge.

1993. *Bodies That Matter: On the Discursive Limits of "Sex."* New York and London: Routledge.

Cannell, Fenella. 1990. "Concepts of Parenthood: the Warnock Report, the Gillick Debate, and Modern Myths," *American Ethnologist* 17 (4): 667–86.

Carrithers, Michael, Steven Collins, and Steven Lukes (eds.). 1985. *The Category of the Person: Anthropology, Philosophy, History*. Cambridge, UK: Cambridge University Press.

Carsten, Janet. 1990. "Women, Men, and the Long and the Short Term of Inheritance in Langkawi, Malaysia," *Bijdragen, tot de Taal-, Land- en Volkenkunde* 146: 270–88.

1995a. "The Substance of Kinship and the Heat of the Hearth: Feeding, Personhood and Relatedness among Malays of Pulau Langkawi," *American Ethnologist* 22 (2): 223–41.

1997. *The Heat of the Hearth: The Process of Kinship in a Malay Fishing Community*. Oxford, UK: Clarendon Press.

(ed.) 2000a. *Cultures of Relatedness: New Approaches to the Study of Kinship*. Cambridge, UK: Cambridge University Press.

2000b. "'Knowing Where You've Come From': Ruptures and Continuities of Time and Kinship in Narratives of Adoption Reunions," *JRAI* 6: 687–703.

Carsten, Janet and Stephen Hugh-Jones. 1995. "Introduction," in Janet Carsten and Stephen Hugh-Jones (eds.), *About the House: Lévi-Strauss and Beyond*. Cambridge, UK: Cambridge University Press.

Collier, Jane and Michelle Z. Rosaldo. 1981. "Politics and Gender in Simple Societies," in Sherry B. Ortner and Hamet Whitehead (eds.), *Sexual Meanings*. Cambridge, UK: Cambridge University Press.

Bibliography

Cussins, Charis. 1997. "Quit Snivelling Cryo-Baby; We'll Decide Which One's Your Mama," in Robbie Davis-Floyd and Joseph Dumit (eds.), *Cyborg Babies: From Techno Tots to Techno Toys.* New York: Routledge.

    1998. "Producing Reproduction: Techniques of Normalization and Naturalization in Infertility Clinics," in Sarah Franklin, and Helena Ragoné (eds.), *Reproducing Reproduction: Kinship, Power, Technological Innovation.* Philadelphia, PA: University of Pennsylvania Press.

Daniel, E. Valentine. 1984. *Fluid Signs: Being a Person the Tamil Way.* Berkeley, CA: University of California Press.

Das, Veena. 1995a. "National Honor and Practical Kinship: Unwanted Women and Children," in Faye D. Ginsburg and Rayna Rapp (eds.), *Conceiving the New World Order: The Global Politics of Reproduction.* Berkeley, CA: University of California Press.

    1995b. "The Anthropology of Pain," in *Critical Events: An Anthropological Perspective on Contemporary India.* New Delhi: Oxford University Press.

Delaney, Carol. 1986. "The Meaning of Paternity and the Virgin Birth Debate," *Man* 21 (3): 494–513.

    1995. "Father, State, Motherland, and the Birth of Modern Turkey," in Sylvia Yanagisako and Carol Delaney (eds.), *Naturalizing Power: Essays in Feminist Culturalist Analysis.* New York and London: Routledge.

Dolgin, Janet L. 1995. "Family Law and the Facts of Family," in Sylvia Yanagisako and Carol Delaney (eds.), *Naturalizing Power: Essays in Feminist Culturalist Analysis.* New York and London: Routledge.

    1997. *Defining the Family: Law, Technology, and Reproduction in an Uneasy Age.* New York: New York University Press.

Dumont, Louis. 1977. *From Mandeville to Marx.* Chicago, IL: University of Chicago Press.

    1980. *Homo Hierarchicus: The Caste System and Its Implications,* 2nd edition, translated by M. Sainsbury, Louis Dumont, and Basia Gulati. Chicago, IL: Chicago University Press.

    1985. "A Modified View of Our Origins: The Christian Beginnings of Modern Individualism," in Michael Carrithers, Steven Collins, and Steven Lukes (eds.), *The Category of the Person: Anthropology, Philosophy, History.* Cambridge, UK: Cambridge University Press.

Edwards, Jeannette. 1993. "Explicit Connections: Ethnographic Enquiry in North-West England," in Jeannette Edwards, et al., *Technologies of Procreation: Kinship in the Age of Assisted Conception.* Manchester, UK: Manchester University Press.

    2000. *Born and Bred: Idioms of Kinship and New Reproductive Technologies in England.* Oxford, UK: Oxford University Press.

Edwards, Jeannette and Marilyn Strathern. 2000. "Including Our Own," in J. Carsten (ed.), *Cultures of Relatedness: New Approaches to the Study of Kinship.* Cambridge, UK: Cambridge University Press.

Edwards, Jeannette, Sarah Franklin, Eric Hirsch, Frances Price, and Marilyn Strathern. 1993. *Technologies of Procreation: Kinship in the Age of Assisted Conception.* Manchester, UK: Manchester University Press.

Engels, Frederick. 1972 [1884]. *The Origin of the Family, Private Property and the State.* London: Lawrence and Wishart.

Errington, Shelly. 1989. *Meaning and Power in a Southeast Asian Realm.* Princeton, NJ: Princeton University Press.

1990. "Recasting Sex, Gender and Power: A Theoretical and Regional Overview," in Jane Atkinson and Shelly Errington (eds.), *Power and Difference: Gender in Island Southeast Asia.* Stanford, CA: Stanford University Press.

Etienne, Mona and Eleanor Leacock. 1980. *Women and Colonization.* New York: Praeger.

Evans-Pritchard, E. E. 1940. *The Nuer: A Description of the Modes of Livelihood and Political Institutions of a Nilotic People.* Oxford, UK: Oxford University Press.

1951. *Kinship and Marriage Among the Nuer.* Oxford, UK: Oxford University Press.

Faubion, James F. (ed.). 2001. *The Ethics of Kinship: Ethnographic Enquiries.* Lanham, MD, and Oxford, UK: Rowan and Littlewood.

Finkler, Kaja. 2000. *Experiencing the New Genetics: Family and Kinship on the Medical Frontier.* Philadelphia, PA: University of Pennsylvania Press.

Fortes, Meyer. 1949. *The Web of Kinship Among the Tallensi: The Second Part of an Analysis of the Social Structure of a Trans-Volta Tribe.* London: Oxford University Press.

1953. "The Structure of Unilineal Descent Groups." *American Anthropologist* 55. Reprinted in Meyer Fortes, 1970. *Time and Social Structure and Other Essays.* London: Athlone Press.

1958. "Introduction," in J. Goody (ed.), *The Developmental Cycle in Domestic Groups.* Cambridge, UK: Cambridge University Press.

1961. "Pietas in ancestor worship," *JRAI* 91: 166–91.

1969. *Kinship and the Social Order.* Chicago, IL: Aldine.

1983. *Oedipus and Job in West African Religion,* reissue edition. Cambridge, UK: Cambridge University Press.

1987a. "The Concept of the Person," in *Religion, Morality and the Person: Essays on Tallensi Religion.* Cambridge, UK: Cambridge University Press, 1987.

1987b. "Divination: Religious Premises and Logical Techniques," in *Religion, Morality and the Person: Essays on Tallensi Religion.* Cambridge, UK: Cambridge University Press.

Bibliography

Fortes, Meyer and E. E. Evans-Pritchard (eds.). 1940. *African Political Systems.* Oxford, UK: Oxford University Press.

Foucault, Michel. 1978. *The History of Sexuality*, Vol. 1. Harmondsworth, UK: Penguin.

Fowler, Henry Watson. 1965. *Fowler's Modern English Usage*, 2nd edition, revised by Sir Ernest Gowers. Oxford, UK: Oxford University Press.

Fox, James J. 1987. "The House as a Type of Social Organisation on the Island of Roti," in C. Macdonald (ed.), *De la Hutte au Palais: Societes "à Maison" en Asie du Sud-Est Insulaire.* Paris: Editions du CNRS.

Fox, Renee C. and Judith P. Swazey. 1978. *The Courage to Fail.* Chicago, IL: Chicago University Press.

Franklin, Sarah. 1993. "Making Representations: The Parliamentary Debate on the Human Fertilisation and Embryology Act," in Jeannette Edwards, et al., *Technologies of Procreation: Kinship in the Age of Assisted Conception.* Manchester, UK: Manchester University Press.

1997. *Embodied Progress: A Cultural Account of Assisted Conception.* London: Routledge.

1998. "Making Miracles: Scientific Progress and the Facts of Life," in Sarah Franklin and Helena Ragoné (eds.), *Reproducing Reproduction: Kinship, Power, Technological Innovation.* Philadelphia, PA: University of Pennsylvania Press.

2001. "Biologization Revisited: Kinship Theory in the Context of the New Biologies," in Sarah Franklin and Susan McKinnon (eds.), *Relative Values: Reconfiguring Kinship Studies.* Durham, NC, and London: Duke University Press.

Franklin, Sarah and Susan McKinnon. 2001a. "Introduction: Relative Values: Reconfiguring Kinship Studies," in Sarah Franklin and Susan McKinnon (eds.), *Relative Values: Reconfiguring Kinship Studies.* Durham, NC, and London: Duke University Press.

(eds.). 2001b. *Relative Values: Reconfiguring Kinship Studies.* Durham, NC, and London: Duke University Press.

Franklin, Sarah and Helena Ragoné (eds.). 1998. *Reproducing Reproduction: Kinship, Power, Technological Innovation.* Philadelphia, PA: University of Pennsylvania Press.

Freeman, Derek. 1979. *Report on the Iban.* London: Athlone Press.

Fulton, J., R. Fulton, and R. G. Simmons. 1977. "The Cadaver Donor and the Gift of Life," in R. G. Simmons, S. D. Klein and R. L. Simmons (eds.), *The Gift of Life.* New York: John Wiley and Sons.

Galvin, Kathy-Lee. 2001. "Schneider Revisited: Sharing and Ratification in the Construction of Kinship," in Linda Stone (ed.), *New Directions in Anthropological Kinship.* Lanham, MD: Rowman and Littlewood.

Gillis, John. 1985. *For Better, for Worse: British Marriages, 1600 to the Present*. New York: Oxford University Press.

　1997. *A World of Their Own Making: A History of Myth and Ritual in Family Life*. Oxford, UK: Oxford University Press.

Ginsburg, Faye D. and Rayna Rapp. 1991. "The politics of reproduction," *Annual Review of Anthropology*, 20: 311–43.

　(eds.). 1995. *Conceiving the New World Order: The Global Politics of Reproduction*. Berkeley, CA: University of California Press.

Good, Anthony. 1991. *The Female Bridegroom: A Comparative Study of Life Crisis Rituals in South India and Sri Lanka*. Oxford, UK: Clarendon Press.

　2000. "Power and Fertility: Divine Kinship in South India," in Monika Böck and Aparna Rao (eds.), *Culture, Creation, and Procreation: Concepts of Kinship in South Asian Practice*, Oxford, UK: Berghahn Books.

Goody, Jack. 1983. *The Development of the Family and Marriage in Europe*. Cambridge, UK: Cambridge University Press.

　1990. *The Oriental, the Ancient and the Primitive: Systems of Marriage and the Family in Preindustrial Societies of Eurasia*. New York: Cambridge University Press.

Gregory, Christopher A. 1982. *Gifts and Commodities*. London: Academic Press.

Gudeman, Stephen and Alberto Rivera. 1990. *Conversations in Colombia*. Cambridge, UK: Cambridge University Press.

Haraway, Donna J. 1989. *Primate Visions: Gender, Race and Nature in the World of Modern Science*. London: Free Association Books.

　1991. *Simians, Cyborgs and Women: The Reinvention of Nature*. London: Free Association Books.

　1997. *Modest_Witness@Second_Millenium.FemaleMan_Meets_OncoMouse: Feminism and Technoscience*. New York, London: Routledge.

Harris, Olivia. 1981. "Households as Natural Units," in K. Young, C. Wolkowitz, and R. McCullagh (eds.), *Of Marriage and the Market*. London: CSE.

Hayden, Corrinne. 1995. "Gender, Genetics, and Generation: Reformulating Biology in Lesbian Kinship," *Cultural Anthropology* 10 (1): 41–63.

Herlihy, David. 1985. *Medieval Households*. Cambridge, UK: Cambridge University Press.

Herzfeld, Michael. 1987. *Anthropology through the Looking-Glass: Critical Ethnography in the Margins of Europe*. Cambridge, UK: Cambridge University Press.

　1997. *Cultural Intimacy: Social Poetics in the Nation-State*. New York: Routledge.

Holy, Ladislav. 1996. *Anthropological Perspectives on Kinship*. London: Pluto Press.

Howell, Signe and Marit Melhuus. 1993. "The Study of Kinship; The Study of Person; A Study of Gender?" in Teresa del Valle (ed.), *Gendered Anthropology*. London and New York: Routledge.

Bibliography

Hugh-Jones, Stephen. 1995. "Inside-out and Back-to-Front: The Androgynous House in Northwest Amazonia," in Janet Carsten and Stephen Hugh-Jones (eds.), *About the House: Lévi-Strauss and Beyond.* Cambridge, UK: Cambridge University Press.

Inden, Ronald B. and Ralph W. Nicholas. 1977. *Kinship in Bengali Culture.* Chicago, IL: Chicago University Press.

Janowski, Monica. 1995. "The Hearth-Group, the Conjugal Couple and the Symbolism of the Rice Meal among the Kelabit of Sarawak," in J. Carsten and Stephen Hugh-Jones (eds.), *About the House: Lévi-Strauss and Beyond.* Cambridge, UK: Cambridge University Press.

Jean-Klein, Iris. 2000. "Mothercraft, Statecraft, and Subjectivity in the Palestinian Intifada," *American Ethnologist* 27 (1): 100–27.

2001. "Nationalism and Resistance: The Two Faces of Everyday Activism in Palestine during the Intifada," *Cultural Anthropology* 16 (1): 83–126.

Joyce, Rosemary A. and Susan D. Gillespie. 2000. *Beyond Kinship: Material and Social Reproduction in House Societies.* Philadelphia, PA: University of Pennsylvania Press.

Kahn, Susan Martha. 2000. *Reproducing Jews: A Cultural Acccount of Assisted Conception in Israel.* Durham, NC, and London: Duke University Press.

Karim, Wazir Jahan. 1992. *Women and Culture: Between Malay Adat and Islam.* Boulder, CO: Westview Press.

1995a. "Introduction: Genderising Anthropology in Southeast Asia," in Wazir Jahan Karim (ed.), *"Male" and "Female" in Developing Southeast Asia.* Oxford, UK, and Washington, DC: Berg.

1995b. "Bilateralism and Gender in in Southeast Asia," in Wazir Jahan Karim (ed.), *"Male" and "Female" in Developing Southeast Asia.* Oxford, UK, and Washington, DC: Berg.

Konrad, Monica. 1998. "Ova Donation and Symbols of Substance: Some Variations on the Theme of Sex, Gender and the Partible Person," *JRAI* 4 (4): 643–67.

Kroeber, Alfred L. 1909. "Classificatory Systems of Relationship," *JARI* 39: 77–84.

Kuper, Adam. 1988. *The Invention of Primitive Society: Transformations of an Illusion.* London: Routledge.

1999. *Culture: The Anthropologists' Account.* Cambridge, MA: Harvard University Press.

Laderman, Carol. 1983. *Wives and Midwives: Childbirth and Nutrition in Rural Malaysia.* Berkeley, CA: University of California Press.

Lakoff, George and Mark Johnson. 1980. *Metaphors We Live by.* Chicago, IL: University of Chicago Press.

Lambek, Michael. 1993. *Knowledge and Practice in Mayotte: Local Discourses of Islam, Sorcery, and Spirit Possession.* Toronto: University of Toronto Press.

1998. "Body and Mind in Mind, Body and Mind in Body: Some Anthropological Interventions in a Long Conversation," in Michael Lambek and Andrew Strathern (eds.), *Bodies and Persons: Comparative Perspectives from Africa and Melanesia.* Cambridge, UK: Cambridge University Press.

Lambert, Helen. 2000. "Sentiment and Substance in North Indian Forms of Relatedness," in Janet Carsten (ed.), 2000. *Cultures of Relatedness: New Approaches to the Study of Kinship.* Cambridge, UK: Cambridge University Press.

Laqueur, Thomas. 1990. *Making Sex: Body and Gender from the Greeks to Freud.* Cambridge, MA, and London: Harvard University Press.

Laslett, Peter. 1977. *Family Life and Illicit Love in Earlier Generations.* Cambridge, UK: Cambridge University Press.

Latour, Bruno. 1993. *We Have Never Been Modern*, translated by Catherine Porter. London: Harvester Wheatsheaf.

Latour, Bruno and Steve Woolgar. 1986. *Laboratory Life: The Construction of Scientific Facts*, 2nd edition. Princeton, NJ: Princeton University Press.

Leach, E. R. 1967. "Virgin birth," *Proceedings of the Royal Anthropological Institute* 39–49.

Leacock, Eleanor. 1978. "Women's Status in Egalitarian Society: Implications for Social Evolution," *Current Anthropology* 19 (2): 247–75.

Lévi-Strauss, Claude. 1969. *The Elementary Structures of Kinship.* Revised edition translated from the French by James Harle Bell, John Richard von Sturmer, and Rodney Needham (eds.). Boston, MA: Beacon Press.

1983. *The Way of the Masks*, translated by Sylvia Modelski. London: Jonathan Cape.

1987. *Anthropology and Myth: Lectures* 1951–1982. Oxford, UK: Blackwell.

Lounsbury, F. G. 1965. "Another View of the Trobriand Kinship Categories," *American Anthropologist* 67: 142–85.

MacCormack, Carol and Merilyn Strathern (eds.). 1980. *Nature, Culture and Gender: A Critique.* Cambridge, UK: Cambridge University Press.

Macdonald, Charles. (ed.). 1987. *De la Hutte au Palais: Societes "à Maison" en Asie du Sud-Est Insulaire.* Paris: Editions du CNRS.

Malinowski, Bronislaw. 1929. *The Sexual Life of Savages.* New York: Harcourt, Brace and World.

1930. "Parenthood – the Basis of Social Structure," in Victor F. Calverton and Samuel D. Schmalhausen (eds.). *The New Generation: The Intimate Problems of Modern Parents and Children.* London: George Allen & Unwin.

Malkki, Liisa. 1994. "Citizens of Humanity: Internationalism and the Imagined Community of Nations," *Diaspora* 3 (1): 41–69.

Bibliography

Marriott, McKim. 1976. "Hindu Transactions: Diversity without Dualism," in Bruce Kapferer (ed.), *Transactions in Meaning*. Philadelphia, PA: ISHI Publications.

Marriott, McKim and Inden, Ronald. 1977. "Towards an Ethnosociology of South Asian Caste Systems," in Kenneth David (ed.), *The New Wind: Changing Identities in South Asia*. Paris and the Hague: Mouton.

Mauss, Marcel. 1985. "A Category of the Human Mind: The Notion of the Person; the Notion of the Self," translated by W. D. Halls, in Michael Carrithers, Steven Collins, and Steven Lukes (eds.), *The Category of the Person: Anthropology, Philosophy, History*. Cambridge, UK: Cambridge University Press.

McGilvray, Dennis B. 1982. "Mukkuvar Vannimai: Tamil Caste and Matriclan Ideology in Batticaloa, Sri Lanka," in Dennis B. McGilvray (ed.), *Caste Ideology and Interaction*. Cambridge, UK: Cambridge University Press.

McKinley, Robert. 1981. "Cain and Abel on the Malay Peninsula," in Mac Marshall (ed.), *Siblingship in Oceania: Studies in the Meaning of Kin Relations* (ASAO Monographs No. 8). Lanham, MD: University Press of America.

McKinnon, Susan. 1995. "Nourishing Kinship Theory: A Commentary on Weismantel's 'Making Kin,'" *American Ethnologist* 22 (4): 704–6.

2000. "Domestic Exceptions: Evans-Pritchard and the Creation of Nuer Patrilineality and Equality," *Cultural Anthropology* 15 (1): 35–83.

Meillassoux, Claude. 1984. *Maidens, Meal, and Money: Capitalism and the Domestic Community*. Cambridge, UK: Cambridge University Press.

Mitchell, Timothy. 1988. *Colonising Egypt*. Berkeley, CA: University of California Press.

Modell, Judith. 1994. *Kinship with Strangers: Adoption and Interpretations of Kinship in American Culture*. Berkeley, CA: University of California Press.

Moore, Henrietta L. 1988. *Feminism and Anthropology*. Cambridge, UK: Polity Press.

1993. "The Differences Within and the Differences Between," in Teresa del Valle (ed.), *Gendered Anthropology*. London and New York: Routledge.

1994. *A Passion for Difference: Essays in Anthropology and Gender*. Cambridge, UK: Polity Press.

Morgan, Lewis Henry. 1871. *Systems of Consanguinity and Affinity of the Human Family*. Washington, DC: Smithsonian Institution.

1877. *Ancient Society: Researches in the Lines of Human Progress from Savagery through Barbarism to Civilization*. New York: Holt.

Morris, Rosamund C. 1995. "All Made Up: Performance Theory and the New Anthropology of Sex and Gender," *Annual Review of Anthropology* 24: 567–92.

Murdock, George P. 1949. *Social Structure*. New York: Macmillan.

Needham, Rodney. 1971. "Remarks on the Analysis of Kinship and Marriage," in R. Needham (ed.), *Rethinking Kinship and Marriage*. London: Tavistock.

Okely, Judith. 1983. *The Traveller-Gypsies*. Cambridge, UK: Cambridge University Press.

Ong, Aihwa and Michael G. Peletz (eds.). 1995. *Bewitching Women, Pious Men: Gender and Body Politics in Southeast Asia*. Berkeley, CA: University of California Press.

Ortner, Sherry B. 1974. "Is Female to Male as Nature is to Culture?" in Michelle Zimbalist Rosaldo and Louise Lamphere (eds.), *Women, Culture and Society*. Stanford, CA: Stanford University Press.

Ortner, Sherry B. and Harriet Whitehead. 1981. *Sexual Meanings: The Cultural Construction of Gender and Sexuality*. Cambridge, UK: Cambridge University Press.

Östör, Akos, Lina Fruzetti, and Steve Barnett. 1982. "Conclusion," in Akos Östör, Lina Fruzetti, and Steve Barnett (eds.), *Concepts of Person: Kinship, Caste and Marriage in India*. Cambridge, MA, and London: Harvard University Press.

Ouroussoff, Alexandra. 1993. "Illusions of Rationality: False Premises of the Liberal Tradition," *Man* (n.s.) 28: 281–98.

Parkin, Robert. 1997. *Kinship: An Introduction to the Basic Concepts*. Oxford, UK: Blackwell.

Parry, Jonathan. 1989. "The End of the Body," in Michael Feher (ed.), *Fragments for a History of the Body, Part Two*. New York: Zone.

Peletz, Michael G. 1987. "The Exchange of Men in 19th-Century Negeri Sembilan (Malaya)," *American Ethnologist* 14 (3): 449–69.

1995a. "Kinship Studies in Late Twentieth-Century Anthropology," *Annual Review of Anthropology* 24: 343–72.

1995b. "Neither Reasonable nor Responsible: Contrasting Representations of Masculinity in a Malay Society," in Aihwa Ong and Michael Peletz (eds.). *Bewitching Women, Pious Men: Gender and Body Politics in Southeast Asia*. Berkeley, CA: University of California Press.

1996. *Reason and Passion: Representations of Gender in a Malay Society*. Berkeley, CA, and Los Angeles: University of California Press.

2001. "Ambivalence in Kinship since the 1940s," in Sarah Franklin and Susan McKinnon (eds.), *Relative Values: Reconfiguring Kinship Studies*. Durham, NC, and London: Duke University Press.

Pina-Cabral, João de. 1986. *Sons of Adam, Daughters of Eve: The Peasant Worldview of the Alto Minho*. Oxford, UK: Clarendon Press.

Pine, Frances. 1996. "Naming the House and Naming the Land: Kinship and Social Groups in Highland Poland," *JRAI* (n.s.) 2 (2): 443–59.

1999. "Incorporation and Exclusion in the Podhale," in Sophie Day, Michael Stewart, and E. Papataxiarchis (eds.), *Lilies of the Field: Marginal People Who Live for the Moment*. Boulder, CO: Westview Press.

Bibliography

Radcliffe-Brown, A. R. 1950. "Introduction," in A. R. Radcliffe-Brown and Daryll Forde (eds.), *African Systems of Kinship and Marriage*. London: Oxford University Press.

Ragoné, Helena. 1994. *Surrogate Motherhood: Conceptions in the Heart*. Boulder, CO, and Oxford, UK: Westview Press.

Ragoné, Helena and France Winddance Twine. 2000. *Ideologies and Technologies of Motherhood: Race Class Sexuality Nationalism*. New York and London: Routledge.

Rapp, Rayna. 1999. *Testing Women, Testing the Fetus: The Social Impact of Amniocentesis in America*. New York and London: Routledge.

Rosaldo M. 1974. "Women, Culture and Society: A Theoretical Overview," in M. Rosaldo and L. Lamphere (eds.), *Women, Culture and Society*. Stanford, CA: Stanford University Press.

1980. "The Use and Abuse of Anthropology: Reflections on Feminism and Cross-Cultural Understanding," *Signs* 5 (3): 389–417.

Rubin, Gayle. 1975. "The Traffic in Women: Notes on the 'Political Economy' of Sex," in Rayna R. Reiter (ed.), *Toward an Anthropology of Women*. New York and London: Monthly Review Press.

Sacks, Karen. 1979. *Sisters and Wives: The Past and the Future of Sexual Equality*. Westport, CT: Greenwood Press.

Scheffler, H. W. 1972. "Systems of Kin Classification: A Structural Typology," in Priscilla Reining (ed.), *Kinship Studies in the Morgan Centennial Year*. Washington, DC: Anthropological Society of Washington.

Scheffler, Harold W. 1978. *Australian Kin Classification*. Cambridge, UK: Cambridge University Press.

Scheffler, Harold W. and F. G. Lounsbury. 1972. *A Study in Structural Semantics: The Siriono Kinship System*. Englewood Cliffs, NJ: Prentice Hall.

Schneider, David M. 1977. "Kinship, Nationality, and Religion in American Culture: Towards a Definition of Kinship," in Janet L. Dolgin, D. S. Kemnitzer, and David M. Schneider (eds.), *Symbolic Anthropology: A Reader in the Study of Symbols and Meanings*. New York: Columbia University Press.

1980. *American Kinship: A Cultural Account*, 2nd edition. Chicago, IL: University of Chicago Press.

1984. *A Critique of the Study of Kinship*. Ann Arbor, MI: University of Michigan Press.

Schneider, David M. and Richard R. Handler. 1995. *Schneider on Schneider: The Conversion of the Jews and Other Anthropological Stories*. Durham, NC: Duke University Press.

Schrauwers, Albert. 1999. "Negotiating Parentage: The Political Economy of 'Kinship' in Central Sulawesi, Indonesia," *American Ethnologist* 26: 310–23.

Schweitzer, Peter P. (ed.). 2000. *Dividends of Kinship: Meanings and Uses of Social Relatedness.* London and New York: Routledge.

Seccombe, Wally. 1992. *A Millennium of Family Change: Feudalism to Capitalism in Northwestern Europe.* London: Verso.

Simpson, Bob. 1998. *Changing Families: An Ethnographic Approach to Divorce and Separation.* Oxford, UK and New York: Berg.

2001. "Making 'Bad' Deaths 'Good': The Kinship Consequences of Posthumous Conception," *JRAI* (n.s.) 7: 1–18.

Spencer, J. 1995. "Occidentalism in the East: The Uses of the West in the Politics and Anthropology of South Asia," in James G. Carrier (ed.), *Occidentalism: Images of the West.* Oxford, UK: Oxford University Press.

Spiro, Melford E. 1968. "Virgin Birth, Parthenogenesis and Physiological Paternity: An Essay in Cultural Interpretation," *Man* 3: 242–61.

Stewart, Michael. 1997. *The Time of the Gypsies.* Boulder, CO, and Oxford, UK: Westview Press.

Stolcke, Verena. 1993. "Is Sex to Gender as Race Is to Ethnicity?" in Teresa del Valle (ed.), *Gendered Anthropology.* London and New York: Routledge.

Stone, Lawrence. 1977. *The Family, Sex and Marriage in England, 1500–1800.* New York: Harper and Row.

Stone, Linda. 1997. *Kinship and Gender: An Introduction.* Boulder, CO, and Oxford, UK: Westview Press.

(ed.). 2001. *New Directions in Anthropological Kinship.* Lanham, MD: Rowman and Littlewood.

Strathern, Marilyn. 1988. *The Gender of the Gift: Problems with Women and Problems with Society in Melanesia.* Berkeley, CA: University of California Press.

1992a. *After Nature: English Kinship in the Late Twentieth Century.* Cambridge, UK: Cambridge University Press.

1992b. *Reproducing the Future: Essays on Anthropology, Kinship and the New Reproductive Technologies.* Manchester, UK: Manchester University Press.

1992c. "Parts and Wholes: Refiguring Relationships in a Postplural World," in Adam Kuper (ed.), *Conceptualising Society.* London: Routledge.

1993. "Weston, Kath, Families We Choose: Lesbians, Gays, Kinship" [Review], *Man* (n.s.) 28 (1) 195–6.

1996. "Potential Property: Intellectual Property Rights and Property in Persons," *Social Anthropology* 4: 17–32.

1997. "Marilyn Strathern on Kinship" (interview with Marilyn Strathern), *EASA Newsletter* 19: 6–9.

1999a. *Property, Substance and Effect: Anthropological Essays on Persons and Things.* London and New Brunswick, NJ: Athlone Press.

1999b. "Refusing Information," in *Property, Substance and Effect: Anthropological Essays on Persons and Things*. London and New Brunswick, NJ: Athlone Press.

1999c. "The Aesthetics of Substance," in *Property, Substance and Effect: Anthropological Essays on Persons and Things*. London and New Brunswick, NJ: Athlone Press.

Tambiah, Stanley J. 1976. *World Conqueror and World Renouncer*. Cambridge, UK: Cambridge University Press.

Taylor, Janelle. 1998. "Images of Contradiction: Obstetrical Ultrasound in American Culture," in Sarah Franklin, and Helena Ragoné (eds.), *Reproducing Reproduction: Kinship, Power, Technological Innovation*. Philadelphia, PA: University of Pennsylvania Press.

Thomas, Nicholas. 1994. *Colonialism's Culture: Anthropology, Travel and Government*. Oxford, UK: Polity Press.

Thomas, Philip. 1999. "No Substance, No Kinship? Procreation, Performativity and Temanambondro Parent/Child Relations," in Peter Loizos and Patrick Heady (eds.), *Conceiving Persons: Ethnographies of Procreation, Fertility and Growth*. London: Athlone Press.

Thompson, Charis. 2001. "Strategic Naturalization: Kinship in an Infertility Clinic," in Sarah Franklin and Susan McKinnon (eds.), *Relative Values: Reconfiguring Kinship Studies*. Durham, NC: Duke University Press.

Toren, Christina. 1990. *Making Sense of Hierarchy*. London: Athlone Press.

Van Esterik, P. (ed.). 1982. *Women of Southeast Asia*, Center for Southeast Asian Studies, monograph. De Kalb, IL: Northern Illinois University.

Wagner, R. 1977. "Analogic Kinship: A Daribi Example," *American Ethnologist* 4: 623–42.

Warnock Committee. 1984. *The Warnock Report: Report of the Committee of Inquiry into Human Fertilisation and Embryology*, Cmnd. 9314. London: Her Majesty's Stationery Office.

Watson, Rubie. 1986. "The Named and the Nameless: Gender and Person in Chinese Society," *American Ethnologist* 13: 619–31.

Weiner, Annette B. 1976. *Women of Value, Men of Renown: New Perspectives in Trobriand Exchange*. Austin, TX: University of Texas Press.

Weismantel, Mary. 1988. *Food, Gender and Society in the Ecuadorean Andes*. Philadelphia, PA: University of Pennsylvania Press.

1995. "Making Kin: Kinship Theory and Zumabagua Adoptions," *American Ethnologist* 22 (4): 685–704.

Weston, Kath. 1991. *Families We Choose: Lesbians, Gays, Kinship*. New York: Columbia University Press.

1995. "Forever is a Long Time: Romancing the Real in Gay Kinship Ideologies," in Sylvia J. Yanagisako and Carol Delaney (eds.), *Naturalizing Power: Essays in Feminist Culturalist Analysis*. New York and London: Routledge.

Wilson, Joni. 2000. "Substantial Connections: The Transacting of Human Organs as a Moral Economy," unpublished Ph.D thesis, University of Edinburgh.

Wolters, O. W. 1982. *History, Culture and Region in Southeast Asian Perspectives*. Singapore: Institute of Southeast Asian Studies.

Yan, Yunxiang. 2001. "Practicing Kinship in Rural North China," in Sarah Franklin and Susan McKinnon (eds.), *Relative Values: Reconfiguring Kinship Studies*. Durham, NC, and London: Duke University Press.

Yanagisako, Sylvia J. 1979. "Family and Household: The Analysis of Domestic Groups," *Annual Review of Anthropology* 8: 161–205.

Yanagisako, Sylvia J. and Jane F. Collier. 1987. "Toward a Unified Analysis of Kinship and Gender," in Jane F. Collier and Sylvia J. Yanagisako (eds.), *Gender and Kinship: Essays towards a Unified Analyis*. Stanford, CA: Stanford University Press.

Yanagisako, Sylvia and Carol Delaney (eds.). 1995. *Naturalizing Power: Essays in Feminist Cultural Analysis*. New York and London: Routledge.

Young, Kate, C. Wolkowitz, and R. McCullagh (eds.). 1981. *Of Marriage and the Market*. London: Routledge and Kegan Paul.

Yuval-Davis, Nira. 1997. *Gender and Nation*. London: Sage Publications.

Index

Index

Austronesian world, 69, 79. *See also*
Vezo of Madagascar

Bachofen, Johan, 58
Bahloul, Joelle, 33
Balkans, 162
Baumann, Gerd, 114–15, 134, 142
Belgium, 2, 99–100
Benares, 119
Berlin, 31
biology, 21, 59, 63–6, 71
birth, 5, 72–3, 72n2, 89
    cultures and, 96–7
    kin, 103, 103n6, 146–53
Bloch, Maurice, xi, 50, 96–7
    "Death and the Concept of the
    Person," xi
blood, 73–4, 127, 137
    relationships, 73–4, 110–16, 139
    substance and, 110, 123–4, 129–31
Blood, Diane, 1–2, 7, 16, 21, 26, 30,
    83, 98–101, 101n4, 105, 105n7,
    107, 107n8, 178–9, 184–6, 188
Blood, Liam, 185
Blood, Stephen, 1–2, 7, 98–101,
    101n4, 184
Bosnia, 158
Bourdieu, Pierre, 24, 48–9, 52–3
    The Logic of Practice, 47
breadmaking, 38–9
Bringa, Tone, 158
British Medical Association, 100
Brown, Sir Stephen, 1, 98–9
Busby, Cecilia, 57, 66, 75–8, 127–8
Butler, Judith, 65
    Bodies That Matter, 65–6
    Gender Trouble, 65

Cannell, Fenella, 168–9
Carrithers, Michael, 86
    "The Concept of the Person," 88
Catholics, 34, 169
celibacy, 17
Chicago, 175
childbirth, 38, 67–8
childrearing, 36, 54
children, 10, 17, 43–4, 185. *See also*
    siblingship
    adopted, 4–7, 21, 26, 83, 103–7,
    103n6, 146–53, 151n3, 184–5
    of artificial insemination, 3,
    101n4, 112–13
    foster, 40, 45, 138–9
    houses and, 44–6, 49
    illegitimate, 159n6
    Malay, 44–6, 72–4, 72n2, 105–6
    Tallensi, 89
China, 28
Christians, 39, 85–6
churches, 53
circumcision, 72–3, 72n2
clanship, 85
cloning, 7, 174, 184
cofeeding, 29
Collier, Jane, 58–9, 62–4, 69–70
Collins, Steven, 86
    "The Concept of the Person,"
    88
colonialism, 12, 36, 51–3
Columbia, 37, 39, 43
commodity exchange, 94–6, 96n2
communities, 23
conception, 23
    posthumous, 7, 96–103, 107
cooking, 35, 37–41, 47–8, 57

Index

feeding, 26, 31, 140
feminists, 8, 20, 60–2
  scholars, 13, 15, 36
  studies, 58–9
fertility, 3, 7–8, 43–4, 170–1, 185
fetus, 40, 123–5, 175–6
Fiji, 51, 53
Finkler, Kaja, 150–1, 151n3
fluids, bodily, 110, 121, 132
food, 39–41, 45, 110, 129–30
forgetting, 17
Fortes, Meyer, 10, 18, 35, 141
  on personhood, 88–91, 91n1, 93
fostering, 45, 137–41
Foucault, Michel, 64, 66
Fowler, H. W., 157–8, 160
France, 12, 33
Franklin, Sarah, xi–xii, 169, 171–3,
  182
  Relative Values: Reconfiguring
  Kinship Studies, xii
Freud Museum, 32n1
Freud, Sigmund, 32n1

gametes, 177
gays, 115, 136, 142, 144–6, 149–50, 161.
  See also lesbians
gazé. *See* non-Gypsies
Geertz, Clifford, 18, 20
gender, 6, 23, 185
  age and, 47–8
  anthropology of, 8, 23, 60–2, 66
  bodies/kinship and, 57–82
  distinctions, 47–9
  feminism and, 20, 58–62
  Hungarian Vlach Gypsies and,
  54, 57, 66–9

kinship and, 11, 20, 23n5, 27–8
Malay and, 57, 71–5, 72n2, 81, 128
marriages and, 46, 58, 72, 76–8
Melanesia and, 70
men/women and, 58
personhood and, 20–2, 127
sex and, 61–6, 69–71, 79–81,
  79n3
in Southeast Asia, 64, 71
space divisions/activities and, 34
studies, 15, 20–2
genetics, 7–8
Germany, 31
gift exchange, 94–6
Gillick, Victoria, 168–9
Gillis, John, 17
GM. *See* crops, genetically modified
  (GM)
Good, Anthony, xii, 117
Gorale region, 53–5
grandmothers, 91
Great Britain, xii, 9, 29, 134, 146, 168,
  184
  artificial insemination in, 1–2, 7,
  21, 26, 98–101, 112–13
  Court of Appeal/High Court of,
  1, 98
  kinship studies of, 12, 17, 153
  Parliament, 171–2
Guardian, The, 99, 101n4
Gudeman, Steve, xi–xii, 39–40, 43,
  164n1
Gypsies of Hungary, 54, 57, 66–9

Haraway, Donna, 22, 166
health care, 3–4, 54
Herzfeld, Michael, 155n5